Individual Rights
Reconsidered

*The Hoover Institution
gratefully acknowledges generous support from*

TAD AND DIANNE TAUBE
TAUBE FAMILY FOUNDATION
KORET FOUNDATION

*Founders of the Program on
American Institutions and Economic Performance*

and Cornerstone gifts from

SARAH SCAIFE FOUNDATION

PHILOSOPHIC REFLECTIONS ON A FREE SOCIETY

Individual Rights Reconsidered

Are the Truths of the U.S. Declaration of Independence Lasting?

Edited by
Tibor R. Machan

HOOVER INSTITUTION PRESS

Stanford University   Stanford, California

www.hoover.org

Hoover Institution Press Publication No. 485

First printing, 2001
07 06 05 04 03 02 01   9 8 7 6 5 4 3 2

Manufactured in the United States of America
The paper used in this publication meets the minimum requirements of American National Standard for Information Sciences—Permanence of Paper for Printed Library Materials, ANSI Z39.48–1984. ♾

Library of Congress Cataloging-in-Publication Data
Individual rights reconsidered : are the truths of the U.S. Declaration of Independence lasting? / edited by Tibor R. Machan.
    p.   cm. — (Philosophic reflections on a free society)
(Hoover Institution Press publication; 485)
    Includes bibliographical references and index.
    ISBN 0-8179-9932-9 (alk. paper)
    1. Individualism. 2. Human rights. 3. Liberalism—United States.
4. United States. Declaration of Independence. I. Machan, Tibor R.
II. Series. III. Hoover Institution Press publication; 485.
JC571 .I4873 2001
323—dc21   00-053899

CONTENTS

ACKNOWLEDGMENTS

I WISH to express my gratitude to the Hoover Institution on War, Revolution and Peace and its director, John Raisian, for generously supporting the publication of this work. Heartfelt thanks also go to Joanne and Johan Blokker for their generous support of the Hoover Institution Press series, Philosophic Reflections on a Free Society. I also wish to thank the contributing authors for their cooperation, patience, and conscientiousness throughout the entire publishing process. Thanks also to Jennifer Beattie at Chapman University for her tireless help in preparing this volume. Let me also thank Pat Baker, Ann Wood, and Marshall Blanchard of the Hoover Institution Press for their extensive and very helpful assistance with the publication of this volume.

T.R.M.

The Hoover Institution
gratefully acknowledges
the support of
JOANNE AND JOHAN BLOKKER
on this project.

CONTRIBUTORS

TIBOR R. MACHAN is Distinguished Fellow and Freedom Communications Professor of Business Ethics and Free Enterprise at the Leatherby Center for Entrepreneurship and Business Ethics, Argyros School of Business and Economics, Chapman University, and a Research Fellow at the Hoover Institution.

RONALD HAMOWY is Professor Emeritus of Intellectual History at the University of Alberta. He is the editor and annotator of the complete edition of Trenchard and Gordon's *Cato's Letters* and has published on eighteenth-century Anglo-American political and social theory.

ERIC MACK is Professor of Philosophy at Tulane University where he is also a member of the faculty of the Murphy Institute of Political Economy. He has edited two books, Auberon Herbert's *The Right and Wrong of Compulsion by the State and Other Essays* and Herbert Spencer's *Man versus the State and Other Essays*. He has published about seventy articles in scholarly journals and anthologies on such topics as the nature and foundation of moral rights, property rights, economic justice, and liberalism and pluralism.

TOM G. PALMER is Fellow in Social Thought at the Cato Institute. He is author of *Learning about Liberty* (Cato Institute, 1997) and *Philanthropy in Central and Eastern Europe: A Resource Book for Foundations, Corporations, and Individuals* (Institute for Humane Studies, 1989).

DOUGLAS B. RASMUSSEN is Professor of Philosophy at St. John's University, Jamaica, New York. He has co-authored *The Catholic Bishops and the Economy: A Debate* (Transaction Books, 1987); *Liberty and Nature: An Aristotelian Defense of Liberal Order* (Open Court, 1991); *Liberalism Defended: The Challenge of Post-Modernity* (Edward Elgar, 1997); and has co-edited *Liberty for the Twenty-First Century* (Roman & Littlefield, 1995). He has published numerous articles and guest-edited *The Monist*, "Teleology and the Foundation of Value" (January 1992).

Individual Rights

Tibor R. Machan

THE U.S. DECLARATION OF INDEPENDENCE states that "We hold these truths to be self-evident; that all men are created equal; that they are endowed by their creator with certain unalienable rights; that among these are life, liberty, and the pursuit of happiness." Let me just focus on the first part of that statement, the claim that "we hold these truths to be self-evident."

Many people, especially critics of the American political framework have said, "Now wait a minute! Clearly it is not self-evident that we are created equal and have those rights. We don't just know any of this without serious argument, evidence, or whatever must be adduced to show these matters to be so. The Founders were clearly wrong to think such ideas to be self-evident."

Yet, notice the phrasing. It is "we *hold* these truths to be self-evident." It suggests that the Founders did that only for the purpose of making their declaration. They were not naïve or inept. They didn't think that anybody who is born comes to know these matters. For purposes of political declarations of the sort they were issuing, it makes sense to think: "On this occasion we're not going to debate this issue, we're simply going to affirm it, to declare to the rest of the world our loyalty to these principles. That doesn't mean that we don't need John Locke's or the Adam Smith's or someone else's intellectual, philosophical, historical, and related studies to show that these rights actually exist, that they are valid ideas. Our document, however, isn't a treatise but a declaration. We want the world to know we are taking a stand."

Those contributing to this volume, however, have as their task not making declarations but considering whether and why a declaration such as the Founders of the American republic produced might be true. They are not Founders of a new country, the principles of which are an important message to the world. They want to be sure that these ideas are actually sound, true.

All who take the individual rights position seriously, even if disagreeing with it, have an interest in seeing what is the case for this position. Why is it to be treated as true rather than as false or a bit of confusion?

There really are quite a few influential and sincere people who do believe that what the Founders declared to be so is false or at best seriously confused. There are some, for example, who maintain that the notion that individuals have basic rights to their lives, liberties, the pursuit of their happiness (or to property[1]) is an invention at a particular historical point. Karl Marx suggested this idea, in his posthumously published book *Grundrisse*, where he noted that such figures as Adam Smith and David Ricardo adopted these ideas with the result that they motivated the historical movement of capitalist productivity.[2] The idea amounts to an unconscious rationalization that would allow certain people—the ruling classes or the bourgeoi-

---

1. Some dispute that Jefferson and his colleagues construed the right to property as one of the unalienable rights of individuals. There is ample evidence, however, showing that this is just how they saw it. See, for example, Luigi Marco Bassani, "Property and Happiness in Thomas Jefferson's Political Thought," paper presented at the 6th Austrian Scholars Conference, Auburn, Ala., March 24–26, 2000.

2. Karl Marx, *Grundrisse* (New York: Harper & Row, 1970), p. 16. "The individual and isolated hunter or fisher who forms the starting point with Smith and Ricardo belongs to the insipid illusions of the eighteenth century."

sie—to gain power or the upper hand. Thus the idea of individual rights is regarded, as the saying goes in academe, as part of an ideology.

Now, "ideology" is often used to mean some simplified philosophy, but here it's a technical term. It means, basically, an invented set of ideas to rationalize political and economic power by some over others. It is akin to when one who wants to play golf because he or she just likes doing so doesn't say that. Instead the reason given is something that seems more respectable, such as that it is good exercise. If, however, one just plays for the pleasure of it, there might well be other, more important things for one to do instead. Exercise, however, sounds important.

Analogously, if there really existed individual rights—for example, to the pursuit of happiness—the Marxists and their kin will claim, that would justify such activities as seeking to enrich oneself in exploitative trade.[3] Even if there are no such rights but one does seek to prosper, the fiction that one has those rights will make what is clearly an undertaking with dubious motives look like a legitimate one. (Oddly enough, even Adam Smith seemed to regard the goal of self-enrichment less than morally noble. He wrote, after all, that "It is not from the benevolence of the butcher, the brewer, or the baker, that we expect our dinner, but from their regard to their own interest. We address ourselves, not to their humanity to their self-love, and never talk to them of our own necessities but of their advantages."[4])

3. Karl Marx said that "the right of man to property is the right to enjoy his possessions and dispose of the same arbitrarily, without regard for other men, independently from society, the right of selfishness." Karl Marx, *Selected Writings*, ed. David McLellan (Oxford: Oxford University Press, 1977), in "On the Jewish Question," p. 53. So what really lies behind the claim to having the right to property is simply selfishness, nothing truly worthwhile. Of course, Marx, who saw society or humanity as the locus of values, did not regard the enhancement of the life of individuals *per se* as something worthwhile, only self-indulgent.

4. Adam Smith, *The Wealth of Nations* (Indianapolis, Ind.: Liberty Classics, 1991), pp. 26–27.

This is a very important way that many intellectuals have dismissed the idea of individual rights as a historical invention, an excuse for a certain class of people to do certain things at the expense, usually, of other classes.[5]

Another criticism, not unrelated to the previous one but distinctive enough to be worth mentioning, is that individual rights are a mistake because there really aren't any individuals. If you study the human race, all you will find is different kinds of collectivities.

We will find tribes, clans, ethnic groups, nations, families, or maybe all of humanity. These constitute beings and human individuals are, as it were, just cells in this being's body. Individuals are to the tribe or some other collective what one's fingers, nose, or eyes are to oneself. The claim is that we are not really whole beings as individuals but instead that we belong to a larger whole or body— the state, the nation, the tribe, whatever.

This line of criticism is especially interesting because there is some plausibility to it. It's very difficult to imagine individuals existing independently of other individuals, independently of their families, neighbors, communities, and so on. We usually do in a sense belong to a community, tribe, nation, and so on. But when this is noted by critics of the individual rights position that forms the philosophical background to the American political tradition, the belonging involved is supposed to be analogous to how an ant belongs to its colony. It looks as if we have there a million or so individual ants, but it's actually the colony that is the significant being in question.

A lot of prominent thinkers maintain and eagerly teach and preach that there are a great many other ways of looking at human lives that are much more sensible than the idea that individuals are sovereign beings with rights. From this latter idea it would follow that individual human beings may not be taken against their own will to serve ends

---

5. The most direct claim to this effect was made by C. B. Macpherson, *The Political Theory of Possessive Individualism* (London: Oxford University Press, 1962).

that are not their own, ones they did not consent to serve. If, however, one belongs to another whole, as a finger to one's body, clearly sometimes the finger may have to be "conscripted" to serve certain purposes, even perhaps not its normal purposes. Richard Harris, the Welsh actor, once broke his nose and then had an operation to remove bone from his hip to replace the bone in his nose so as to save his looks. The hipbone had no rights against this. Many of the critics of the American political tradition charge that the claim that there exist individual rights is just as absurd as the claim that hip or finger rights exist.

That's another one of the reasons that arguments are needed to establish the existence of individual human rights—namely, that the existence of individual human beings is seriously denied by many influential intellectuals. Thus we aren't justified just saying that we hold the existence of individual rights to be self-evident. As such their existence would fail to be demonstrated.

The way human beings go about deciding many issues, including political ones, is by trying to figure out which answer to a problem can be substantiated or well supported. Of course, often we don't have extensive time to think through these kinds of issues, so we just work with what we inherit from our elders, what is dominant in our cultures, and so on. Still, now and then—and for some of our specialists like political philosophers—it is crucial to investigate what idea about politics makes the best sense.

This is what our contributors have attempted to do in most of their work, including in their essays for this volume. They have spent time looking into the comparative merits of political ideas and have come to the conclusion that America's original and essentially libertarian political stance, based on individual rights, has a great deal of merit and stands up successfully to its challengers.

I shall only go a little distance to begin our exploration. I will try to show that the individual rights position is at least plausible. To begin with, notice, as you read these lines, what you're doing and what I'm doing. This may be thought of as a minor but telling experiment. What can be noticed on the spot is that we are both, to some measure, creative beings.

A reader is evaluating what a writer is doing—whether the writer is using the best expressions, repeating himself, employing biased language, suppressing some points and overplaying others. All these and other questions bring into play certain standards that we are using to judge ourselves and others, and the use of which assumes we have a choice in how we act.

In other words, we normally see ourselves as creative and responsible agents. We are not just following prompters or responding to stimuli. Instead, a reader might ask, "What question might I pose to this writer? What might be doubtful and something to which I should object? What is missing in the argument with which I am confronted?" In short, here we are being active, creative agents, doing some creative thinking on our own initiative.

How does this relate to the issue of basic individual rights? It gives evidence of our individuality, consisting here of our capacity to take the initiative and create something on our own. Of course, a lot of creative potential goes to waste. But the issue here is whether such a creative potential is real. I think any reader can answer that in the affirmative because self-observation will demonstrate it. The individual is individuated in part by virtue of doing something original on his or her own.

None of this denies our social nature, however. We do normally utilize much that is given to us by others. The bulk of the language we use, for example, we did not create ourselves. A poet—to focus on a clear and somewhat easy case—does, however, regularly put the language together differently, and so does everyone once in a while, not to mention editorialists, novelists, song writers, and so on. We can all use language, which is often said to be a purely social product, in creative and idiosyncratic ways. That is a uniquely human capacity and marks us as essentially individuals.

That is also one of the reasons we differ from other animals in the world. We are not just operating by instinct. We have to make an effort all the time to exert ourselves and meet the next challenge we face in our lives. This is something that is not just going to happen, without effort, without initiative. Sure, some of us can get along by simply riding on the accomplishments of others if they are foolish or kind enough to allow this. Yet somebody has to go to bat and get things accomplished. We have to take on the responsibility of, as it were, making a life. This is a uniquely human element in us. It is evident in the smallest measure of human action. We have to do something of our own choice. We have to initiate action. We can initiate it with a lot of aid from others, but that aid would not amount to very much unless we put it to constructive, productive, creative use.

I submit that here we encounter a fundamental fact about human beings. It is not a fact that is explainable by our membership in tribes, nor in families, states, ethnic or racial groups, or the like. This is something that we do as individual human beings. It is also what explains a lot of odd things about human life, which you cannot find in many other kinds of lives. Being wrong is not a problem that mice or geese have. If they have to fly south, they'll fly south. It is not as if they conducted a debate on such matters, as people often do. Other animals do not embark upon that kind of activity.

One of the reasons human beings constantly remake society is this capacity for individual initiative. Human beings tend, in every successive generation, to do something novel. Sometimes uselessly new, but it's almost like a clear definition of human life to reinvent humanity.

This misleads some people into believing that there is nothing stable about human life because so many people are fascinated with the human ability to change—sometimes, indeed, to the point of ruin. Especially as adolescents, they want to be creative and pay little attention to anything that is traditional, well tried, and true.

We have here a vital human capacity to do things with our lives according to our own critical capacities. It doesn't take a rocket scientist to move from here to the next point, that when we are amongst other human beings we can have this capacity undermined by our social interactions. Some people will rob, try to kidnap, assault, tyrannize, oppress, murder us, and so on, which means that what it is to be us, human beings, is at risk—as well as can benefit enormously from being—within human communities. In order to be with others who can be extremely valuable to and are the source of so many of the wonders of our lives, we also have to make sure that there are certain terms that they do not breach.

Let me elaborate this a bit. We all know that in our own interaction with our friends, family, and colleagues there are some limits. If certain conditions are not met, the relationship is terminated. Although these terms in personal relationships vary a great deal, they do suggest clearly enough that not anything goes between parties to such relationships.

In the larger picture of social life, there are basic terms, as well, usually pertaining to how suitable the society is to human survival and flourishing. The most fundamental condition proposed by those in the American political tradition is the basic sovereignty of citizens. That is, each person's sovereignty—his or her creative, self-governing, and inventive nature—must be respected and, if need be, competently protected. This is indispensable for civilized social life.

The basic conditions arise from the crucial human element in each of us, one that needs to be guarded against abuse, invasion, tyranny, and oppression. The idea that each person has basic individual rights amounts to putting up signs to warn people that we are individuals and may not be used against our own judgment. It signals everyone that we are our own masters of our own lives, that we are self-governors.

This is what the notion of the consent of the governed comes to, most fundamentally. One may be governed but not against one's own consent. In simple professional relationships, this is clearly evident: One may be put to sleep by one's dentist, he can dig in one's mouth at great length, but he first had to get authorization. If he just proceeded without such authorization, he would be a criminal.

The rights that the contributors to this volume will consider—to life, liberty, property, and derivative rights such as freedom of contract and so on—spell out the conditions of a truly human community. The laws of such a community are supposedly laid out, in greater and greater detail down to some minuscule things that only lawyers understand with their small print, that the individual—not somebody else—is the ultimate authority over what happens to him or her.

It is worth noticing, too, that this is the respect in which, as the U.S. Declaration states, we are equal. Not in how tall, beautiful, smart, or rich our parents or we are. Those are not what equality is about because, for one, such equality could not even be attempted without massive violation of individual sovereignty. No, the equality at issue means that we all, as human beings, have these rights. We are all in charge of our lives, and others don't get to run them for us unless we permit it.

That is the equality that is crucial in the American political and legal tradition, rather than what is proposed in the egalitarian tradition—namely, equality of condition or even equality of opportunity. Not everyone can have an equal opportunity to be a jockey or a basketball player, given his or her particular attributes. The notion that everyone must have an equal opportunity to attain anything is impossible.

What does make clear sense is that wherever possible one's life ought to be under one's own jurisdiction, that one must have ultimate personal authority to run it. This is also what the international human rights movement rests on, an implicit understanding that this idea of politics and law applies wherever there are human communities.

Although such regimes may not be brought about by force of arms or very quickly, it is, nevertheless, a universally good idea. As long as human beings are concerned, they must be viewed as makers of themselves, as creators, developers of their talents, and so on—in short, masters over their own but not other's lives. This is the response to those who have dismissed individual rights as mere historical fiction, fitted only to the facilitation of certain class interest and rule, rather than as principles that ought to guide community life in any era, everywhere.

The main reason that in the American political tradition there is so much concern with individual liberty is that within that tradition the importance of the human individual is supposed to be fully acknowledged. The right to individual liberty is the condition that one enjoys when people respect and treat one as a creative, productive, freely choosing kind of being rather than a tool for others to use at their discretion.

There are certain phrases bandied about these days that would especially disturb anybody who appreciates the above points. Consider, for example, the claim often made—namely, that "children are our most important resource." This suggests, in a uniquely modern fashion, that children are resources for us—the state, family, community, nation, or even race. This language vis-à-vis a human being signals quite clearly that something important about human life is being forgotten—that individuals are the masters of their own lives and that those lives are not available for others without having obtained the individual's permission. A person must be asked for his or her cooperation, service, and help and must not be conscripted to pursue objectives that have not become one's own.

In the criminal law, one will occasionally still hear references to the importance of this idea. For example, we stress the importance of due process as we confront apprehending and convicting criminals. Why? The reason is that unless certain terms are respected and protected, under which citizens must be treated, their basic nature as human beings will not be accommodated. To put it differently, the system will then fail to be just. Their creative, productive nature as choosing agents would be violated if other persons or institutions dealt with them as a resource there for the picking.

The most vital element of classical liberalism, the philosophical foundation of the American political tradition, is that the individual is the locus of value in a human community. Of course, other things have value, too, but derivatively. It's the individual human being who has primary value.

There's a moral tradition, however, that makes it difficult to pro-claim that the individual human being—referring, of course, to one-self as well as to everyone else—is most important. Most people feel that way, intuitively, but it's very difficult to assert it as a thesis. It sounds selfish, it appears to exhibit hubris or vanity. It prompts such questions as, "Who do you think you are? Why are you being so selfish?" Those questions are difficult to address. Politically, when one affirms the importance of individuals, very quickly the objection is raised, "Do you mean that you're important? What makes you so important? What about the greater good of the community, the na-tion, humanity? You are being selfish, aren't you."

People tend to be intimidated by this kind of questioning—psy-chologically, philosophically, and socially—and disguise what they really ought to affirm without hesitation. It is difficult, however, to come out and say, "I am rightly important to me, and you are impor-tant to you, and so, in a human community, we ought each to be recognized as important."[6] But that is a prerequisite to an effective defense of our liberty. Because if one does not believe that one is important, that one's life is a basic value, how is one going to defend the conditions, namely, individual rights, from others who are threat-ening them? If one holds that "Well, I'm not very important," obvi-

6. See, for more on this, Tibor R. Machan, *Classical Individual, The Supreme Importance of Each Human Being* (London: Routledge, 1998).

ously, those who affirm various projects for which one may be a resource have a prima facie advantage.

If, however, one can keep in mind the basic individualist element of classical liberalism, that every individual human being is an end in himself or herself and not to be used against his or her permission, then the case for liberty is no longer going to be affirmed with hesitation. Indeed, that is why we can make clear sense of why murder, assault, rape, or kidnapping are all evil and to be banned in a civilized community.

If so, however, then why are a lot of other intrusions upon one's life that are often tolerated and unopposed not similarly evil? Indeed, they are. That is because they violate the rights of a human individual who is the kind of being whose proper existence in the community of others requires the respect and protection of those rights.

Alone, or on a desert island, the issue is moot because there's nobody there who could voluntarily, by his or her own volition, make the decision to use another as an unwilling resource. In a community of millions of people—or even just ten—there can always be somebody who wants a shortcut to achieving both important and trivial goals that could use others' assistance.

Take such goals as support of the arts, farming, sport arenas, foreign aid, subsidies for educators and scientists, and the like. Many believe that these important things need to be provided with one's support without asking one's permission. But if one has basic rights to life, liberty, and property, that belief is wrong.

The central point about classical liberalism and the notion of individual rights is that one's life is one's own and that if other people want to deal with someone, they have to ask, convince, and persuade that individual to lend support, to cooperate. This is one of the most civilizing forces in human society: not to permit the use of coercive force by one individual toward another, by one group of people toward others, but to insist that agreements, cooperation, and mutual effort must be reached through consent. People, instead of conquering, expropriating from, or conscripting others to gain their cooperation, must confine themselves to the use of reasoned and peaceful persuasion.

The American Founders gained a clear enough glimpse of these points so as to identify certain basic rights of all individuals by reference to which the norm would have to be to treat persons as ends rather than unwilling means in various communities. In this volume we will explore whether their understanding of the nature of just community life merits continued respect and adherence.

CHAPTER ONE

The Declaration
of Independence

Ronald Hamowy

THE DECLARATION OF INDEPENDENCE is almost certainly the most powerful piece of political rhetoric ever penned. Although written for a specific historical purpose, it nevertheless enunciates a political philosophy that transcends the particularities of time and place and offers a general theory of rights and of the legitimacy of resistance against established authority. Despite its timelessness, however, the Declaration, especially its listing of the grievances against the Crown, are best read against the backdrop of late eighteenth-century North American history.

It is fair to say that when hostilities broke out between the British and Americans at Lexington and Concord in April 1775 few if any colonists supported independence from Great Britain. The First Continental Congress, which had met in Philadelphia during September and October of 1774, had repeatedly reaffirmed the colonies' underlying loyalties to the British Crown once their grievances had

This essay borrows from two previously published articles: "The Declaration of Independence," in Jack P. Greene, ed., *Encyclopedia of American Political History: Studies of the Principal Movements and Ideas*, 4 vols. (New York: Charles Scribner's Sons, 1989): I: 455–65; and "Rights," in Jack P. Greene and J. R. Pole, eds., in *Blackwell's Encyclopedia of the American Revolution* (Cambridge, Mass.: Basil Blackwell, 1991): 682–87.

been redressed. Indeed, a second Congress was to convene in May 1775 only if the colonies continued to find themselves burdened by the oppressive legislation to which they so strenuously objected. Meanwhile, the colonies bound themselves to implement a ban on all imports from Great Britain, to discontinue the slave trade, and to embargo all exports to Britain, Ireland, and the West Indies. This "Continental Association" was met not with offers of conciliation, as many had hoped,[1] but with a policy directed at punishing the colonies for their insubordination.

In February 1775 the British Parliament declared that the colony of Massachusetts was in a state of rebellion, and in the following month King George III endorsed the New England Restraining Act, forbidding the New England colonies from trading with any nation except Britain and prohibiting them from fishing in the North Atlantic. Two weeks later, upon learning that several other colonies had ratified the Continental Association, the Restraining Act was extended to Maryland, New Jersey, Pennsylvania, South Carolina, and Virginia. Yet, despite these measures, the Second Continental Congress, on 5 July 1775, adopted John Dickinson's Olive Branch Petition, which expressed the colonists' earnest hope for reconciliation with the motherland and which called upon the King to work toward

---

1. The Continental Congress had adopted the Declaration and Resolves on 14 October 1774. The document denounced the Coercive Acts and the Quebec Act as offenses against justice and as unconstitutional and condemned as violations the various revenue acts passed by Parliament since 1763. It further characterized the extension of vice admiralty courts, the dissolution of colonial assemblies, and the quartering of British troops in colonial towns in peacetime as violations of the natural and prescriptive rights of Englishmen. The Declaration was laid before Parliament on 19 January, at which time William Pitt, Earl of Chatham, moved that British troops be immediately withdrawn from Boston. Notwithstanding the fact that the vote against this resolution was substantial, Pitt again proposed a reconciliation plan on 1 February, which among other things called for British recognition of the Continental Congress and a pledge that no revenue measure would be levied on the American colonies without the approval of the provincial assemblies. This measure was also defeated by the Lords.

the reestablishment of peace. Even the Declaration of the Causes and Necessities of Taking Up Arms, written by Dickinson and Thomas Jefferson and endorsed by Congress on the day following adoption of the Olive Branch Petition, rejected independence while asserting that the colonists would not be enslaved even at the cost of their lives.

While these formal resolutions were enacted by the Continental Congress, events were quickly moving toward the colonies' formal separation from Great Britain. On 20 December 1775 the Massachusetts Provincial Congress replaced Thomas Cushing, a conservative, with Elbridge Gerry, a radical and follower of Samuel Adams, as a delegate to the Continental Congress, thus securing for the pro-independence forces a majority in the Massachusetts delegation.[2] In March, by which time Gerry had arrived in Philadelphia to take his seat, the Virginia delegation had shifted into the radical camp with the defection of Benjamin Harrison from the conservative to the independence faction and the return to Philadelphia of Richard Henry Lee. The delegations of the two most populous colonies were thus united in supporting independence by the early spring of 1776.

The impetus toward separation was further accelerated by news from Britain. When on 12 September 1775 Congress had reconvened from its summer recess, it learned that George III had refused to receive the Olive Branch Petition and had proclaimed the colonies to be in "open and avowed rebellion." Nor was the King's speech from the throne at the opening of Parliament, delivered on 26 October, any more conciliatory. Despite the colonists' numerous protestations of their continuing loyalty to the Crown, George maintained that "the rebellious war now levied is become more general, and is

---

2. Each colonial delegation to the Continental Congress was given one vote, determined by the majority of its members. John Adams, Samuel Adams, and Elbridge Gerry, who were strong supporters of independence, were thus able to outvote John Hancock and Robert Treat Paine and to control the vote of Massachusetts.

manifestly carried on for the purpose of establishing an independent Empire." In anticipation of the British use of mercenary troops in America the King also alluded to "the most friendly offers of foreign assistance" that he had received.[3] Some months later Congress received the news that Parliament had enacted legislation declaring the colonies beyond the protection of the Crown and prohibiting all trade with them.[4] The Act further authorized the forfeiture of captured American ships and cargoes as enemy property and the impressment of captured crews onto British ships of war. John Adams viewed this action of Parliament as a virtual declaration that the colonies were to be treated as independent of Great Britain, noting that "It may be fortunate that the Act of Independency should come from the British Parliament rather than the American Congress: But it is very odd that Americans should hesitate at accepting such a gift."[5]

Perhaps the single most decisive factor in putting an end to such hesitation was the publication of Thomas Paine's *Common Sense* on 9 January 1776. In what must be regarded as one of the most electrifying political polemics ever written, Paine described the ties that connected the colonists to the mother country as chains that fettered a flourishing people, depriving them of the freedom that was their birthright. No benefit, no advantage nor profit, Paine argued, could be gained from reconciliation with the British monarch, a tyrant

3. Peter Force, *American Archives*, 4th Series, 6 vols. (Washington, D.C.: Under Authority of Congress, 1837–1846): VI: 1–3; quoted in Edward Dumbauld, *The Declaration of Independence* (Norman: University of Oklahoma Press, 1950): 11. In the event, George made treaties with the principalities of Hesse-Cassel, Brunswick, and Hanau, whereby they agreed to furnish troops for Britain's war in America.

4. The Prohibitory Act (16 Geo. III, c. 5), which received the King's signature on 22 December 1775.

5. John Adams to Horatio Gates, 23 March 1776, in Paul H. Smith, ed., *Letters of Delegates to Congress, 1774–1789*, 4 vols. (Washington, D.C.: Library of Congress, 1976–1979): III: 431.

whose hands were already stained with the blood of American patriots. Monarchy, Paine contended, inevitably corrupted those who held political power that, unconstrained, extended itself into every facet of social and economic life. For Paine the legitimate functions of government were simple and few, securing freedom and property and the free exercise of conscience. The enormous complexity of the British government under which the colonists suffered served only to misdirect the colonists from the locus of corruption, the hereditary and far-reaching nature of the Crown. Europe's squabbles were not America's and the corruption endemic to European princes need not be imported to this continent.

> It is repugnant to reason, to the universal order of things, to all examples from the former ages, to suppose that this continent can longer remain subject to any external power. The most sanguine in Britain does not think so. The utmost stretch of human wisdom cannot, at this time, compass a plan short of separation, which can promise the continent even a year's security. Reconciliation is now a fallacious dream. Nature hath deserted the connection, and Art cannot supply her place.[6]

The success of Paine's pamphlet was nothing short of phenomenal. It is reputed to have sold half a million copies,[7] and excerpts appeared in newspapers throughout the colonies. In the crucial days before 4 July it would have been close to impossible for any literate colonist not to have been familiar with the arguments Paine put forward nor to have been unaffected by them. More important, its effects were almost immediate, and the debate between the radicals and those

---

6. Thomas Paine, "Common Sense," in Philip S. Foner, ed., *The Life and Major Writings of Thomas Paine* (Secaucus, N.J.: Citadel Press, 1974): 23.

7. Philip S. Foner, "Introduction: Thomas Paine—World Citizen and Democrat," in Foner, ed., *Life and Writings of Paine*, xiv. Paine himself noted that it sold 120,000 copies within three months of its appearance. "Editor's Introduction," in Thomas Paine, *Common Sense*, Isaac Kramnick, ed. (Hammondsworth, Middlesex: Penguin Books, 1976): 8.

supporting reconciliation that raged throughout the colonial press following its publication tipped decisively toward independence.

By the spring of 1776, the momentum for independence had reached a point where no other course was politically feasible. On 12 April the North Carolina Provincial Congress empowered its delegation to the Continental Congress to support a motion declaring the independence of the colonies from Great Britain. One month later, on 15 May, the Virginia Convention instructed the colony's delegates to propose that Congress "declare the United Colonies free and independent States; absolved from all allegiance to the British Crown or Parliament of Great Britain." The Continental Congress itself had not been inactive during this period. On the same day that the Virginia Convention in Williamsburg was authorizing its delegates to propose independence, the Congress adopted a resolution drafted by John Adams recommending that the colonies assume full powers of government and that all exercise of authority under the Crown be suppressed. Both the North Carolina and Virginia declarations were presented to Congress on the same day, 27 May. Within the next few days Connecticut, New Hampshire, and Delaware all adopted new instructions to their delegations in Philadelphia. Finally, on 7 June, in compliance with the instructions received from Virginia, Richard Henry Lee, the colony's senior delegate, moved, seconded by John Adams, "that these United Colonies are, and of right ought to be, free and independent States, that they are absolved from all allegiance to the British Crown, and that all political connection between them and the State of Great Britain is, and ought to be, totally dissolved."

The conservative opposition in Congress could, by this point, only delay passage of the Lee resolution, but the pro-separatist forces were conscious that a declaration of this sort would have far greater impact were it supported by all the colonies. Consequently, it was agreed that Congress postpone consideration of Lee's motion for three weeks, by which time, it was thought, the middle colonies could be brought into line. As Jefferson remarked in his notes on the proceedings of the Congress, "It appearing in the course of these debates that the colonies of N. York, New Jersey, Pennsylvania, Delaware, Maryland & South Carolina were not yet matured for falling from the parent stem, but that they were fast advancing to that state, it was thought most prudent to wait a while for them, and to postpone the final decision to July 1."[8] There could be little doubt about the ultimate outcome of a vote on the issue, however, and on 11 June Congress appointed a committee to draft a declaration to serve as a preamble to Lee's resolution. The committee consisted of John Adams, Benjamin Franklin, Thomas Jefferson, and Roger Sherman, all of whom were outspoken supporters of independence, and Robert R. Livingston, its sole conservative member. The choice of Jefferson as the senior member of the committee—his name came first in the order of the vote—was particularly felicitous. A writer of remarkable power and great elegance, Jefferson was selected by the committee to prepare a draft of the document, which, as it was to turn out, was presented to the Congress for consideration with only minor alterations.

Jefferson's draft did not, nor was it intended to, offer an original theory of government upon which the colonists were to rely in rebelling against the Crown. In formulating the political principles that underpinned the Revolution—and revolution it certainly was—Jefferson, as he was later to write, sought

> not to find out new principles, or new arguments, never before thought of, not merely to say things which had never been said before; but to place before mankind the common sense of the subject, in terms so plain and firm as to command assent, and to justify ourselves in the independent stand we are compelled to take. Neither aiming at orig-

8. Jefferson, "Notes of Proceedings in the Continental Congress," in *The Papers of Thomas Jefferson*, vol. I, *1760–1776* (Princeton, N.J.: Princeton University Press, 1950): 313.

inality of principle or sentiment, nor yet copied from any particular and previous writing, [the Declaration] was intended to be an expression of the American mind, and to give to that expression the proper tone and spirit called for by the occasion. All its authority rests then on the harmonizing sentiments of the day, whether expressed in conversation, in letters, printed essays, or in the elementary books of public right, such as Aristotle, Cicero, Locke, Sidney, etc.[9]

Indeed, absence of originality of principle can hardly be viewed as legitimate criticism of a document intended to justify to a new nation and to the world the necessity of resorting to arms against a tyrannous government. Jefferson's task was to draft a statement setting forth the justice of the American cause that would prove acceptable not only to himself but to the colonies' delegates assembled in Philadelphia—and, ultimately, to the American people. In doing this, he composed a document that captured the ideological substance of American revolutionary thought, which was grounded in a theory of natural, inalienable rights. It might well be true of the Declaration, as John Adams observed some years later, that "there is not an idea in it but what has been hackneyed in Congress for two years before."[10] But, although meant as criticism, this charge only strengthens one's admiration for Jefferson's handiwork in distilling the revolutionaries' philosophy of government and their political aspirations in so clear and compelling a manner.

The opening paragraph of the Declaration provides the reasons for its publication:

When in the Course of human events, it becomes necessary for one people to dissolve the political bands which have connected them

9. Jefferson to Henry Lee, 8 May 1825, in Paul Leicester Ford, ed., *The Writings of Thomas Jefferson*, 10 vols. (New York: G. P. Putnam's Sons, 1892–1899): X: 343.

10. Adams to Timothy Pickering, 6 August 1822, in Charles Francis Adams, ed., *The Works of John Adams: Second President of the United States*, 10 vols. (Boston: Little, Brown and Company): II: 514.

with another, and to assume among the powers of the earth the separate and equal station to which the Laws of Nature and of Nature's God entitle them, a decent respect to the opinions of mankind requires that they should declare the causes which impel them to the separation.

Jefferson then sets forth the ideological foundations upon which the Revolution was predicated, in which he explicates his references to "the Laws of Nature and of Nature's God":

> We hold these truths to be self-evident, that all men are created equal, that they are endowed by their Creator with certain unalienable Rights, that among these are Life, Liberty and the pursuit of Happiness. That to secure these rights, Governments are instituted among Men, deriving their just powers from the consent of the governed. That whenever any Form of Government becomes destructive of these ends, it is the Right of the People to alter or to abolish it, and to institute new Government, laying its foundation on such principles and organizing its powers in such form, as to them shall seem most likely to effect their Safety and Happiness. Prudence, indeed, will dictate that Governments long established should not be changed for light and transient causes; and accordingly all experience hath shewn, that mankind are more disposed to suffer, while evils are sufferable, than to right themselves by abolishing the forms to which they are accustomed. But when a long train of abuses and usurpations, pursuing invariably the same Object evinces a design to reduce them under absolute Despotism, it is their right, it is their duty, to throw off such Government, and to provide new Guards for their future security.

There follows a catalog of the abuses and usurpations that the colonies had suffered at the hands of the British Crown and from which no redress appeared possible. As important as was the list of grievances, however, it is the document's preamble, which contains the Declaration's political philosophy, that has occupied the close attention of political theorists and intellectual historians since its first appearance.

Almost a commonplace in the last quarter of the eighteenth century, the theory of government propounded in the Declaration bears the indelible imprint of Whig revolutionary thought and particularly of its chief exponent, John Locke.[11] The popularity of Locke's political views among the colonists, both directly through his works and through the large number of political writings that he influenced, was immense. It is not surprising that the sentiments Jefferson expressed—at times even the phrasing he employed—regarding the social contract, the nature of individual rights, and the right to rebellion echoed Locke's *Second Treatise of Government*. Examinations of booksellers' lists and the catalogs of institutional, circulating, and private libraries in the period before 1776 show Locke's works, both philosophical and political, to have been readily accessible to any colonist, as indeed were the other, lesser Whig treatises, particularly Algernon Sidney's *Discourses Concerning Government* and John Trenchard and Thomas Gordon's *Cato's Letters*.[12] Bernard Bailyn, in his definitive analysis of the sources of American revolutionary ideology, has found that "in pamphlet after pamphlet the American writers cited Locke on natural rights and on the social and govern-

11. Locke's influence on Jefferson's Declaration in particular and on American revolutionary thought in general has been called into question by Aldo Tassi, *The Political Philosophy of the American Revolution* (Washington, D.C.: University Press of America, 1978), and Garry Wills, *Jefferson's Declaration of Independence* (Garden City, N.Y.: Doubleday, 1978). Tassi maintains that "a careful examination of [the] alleged connections between Locke's political theory and the American Revolution reveals that they are based on a tissue of unfounded assumptions" (p. 3) and that American political thought during this period was in fact shaped by what appears to be a Rousseau-like concern for political community. Wills contends that Jefferson's Declaration owes little if anything to Locke's political views but can be best analyzed as reflecting the moral and political philosophy of the Scottish Enlightenment. There is no historical warrant for either of these views.

12. David Lundberg and Henry F. May, "The Enlightened Reader in America," *American Quarterly*, 28 (1976): 262–93. For the relation between Locke's political thought and that of Trenchard and Gordon, see Ronald Hamowy, "Cato's Letters, John Locke, and the Republican Paradigm," *The History of Political Thought* XI (1990): 273–94.

mental contract," and that Locke's treatises stood with *Cato's Letters* as "the most authoritative statement of the nature of political liberty."[13] Indeed, if any one political work could be said to capture "the harmonizing sentiments of the day" in the period immediately prior to the American Revolution, it would be Locke's *Second Treatise*.

Although not published until after James II had been successfully deposed, Locke's work on government was actually written some ten years earlier. Peter Laslett has shown that the composition of *The Second Treatise*—at least a substantial portion of it—dates from 1679 to 1680, a decade before the Glorious Revolution. As Laslett notes, the treatise was "a demand for a revolution to be brought about, not the rationalization of a revolution in need of defence,"[14] and, as such, its conclusions respecting the limits of authority of the civil magistrate and the right to revolt against a government that exceeded those limits were particularly apposite. Indeed, the arguments justifying rebellion against a Stuart despot, as put forward by Locke, would serve quite adequately against a Hanoverian or any other tyrant.

The main outlines of Locke's doctrine are clear and unambiguous: All men are by nature free and independent beings, originally constrained solely by the law of nature, that is, the rule of right reason. The state of nature into which men are originally born, although not a pre-social one, is a pre-political one; and although pre-political, mankind's original state is not lawless inasmuch as the law of nature dictates that no man may harm another in his life, health, liberty, or possessions. It further follows from the law of nature that men may be restrained from invading others' rights and may be punished by

13. Bernard Bailyn, *The Ideological Origins of the American Revolution* (Cambridge: Belknap Press of Harvard University Press, 1967): 27, 36.

14. Peter Laslett, "'Two Treatises of Government' and the Revolution of 1688," in John Locke, *Two Treatises of Government*, Peter Laslett, ed. (Cambridge Texts in the History of Political Thought; Cambridge: Cambridge University Press, 1988): 47.

others for doing so. Governments are established solely for the purpose of better protecting the rights with which all men are naturally endowed; the power to protect one's life, liberty, and estate against injury and to judge and punish those who offend against them can be surrendered to the civil magistrate only by individual consent. Once a government acts beyond its trust—the preservation of the lives, liberties, and estates of its subjects—it ceases being legitimate and may no longer command the allegiance of the people. At that point revolution is lawful.

The crucial test of all government, no matter how constituted, lies in whether or not it respects the inalienable rights with which all men are endowed. These rights, Locke maintained, owe their existence neither to convention nor to the presence of a sovereign who, as Hobbes had argued, both created them and made their exercise possible. They are rooted in man's very nature and are unconditional and nontransferable. Men do not, nor can they, compromise them by entering into civil society; nor can these rights be modified in some way to conform to the dictates of the magistrate. The transcendent purpose of government is the preservation of these rights. Locke wrote: "The great and *chief end* therefore, of Mens uniting into Commonwealths, and putting themselves under Government, is the *Preservation of their Property*." And "property," Locke noted in the sentence preceding, refers to men's "Lives, Liberties and Estates."[15] The Declaration affirms this conclusion when it asserts that all men "are endowed by their Creator with certain unalienable Rights, that among these are, Life, Liberty and the pursuit of Happiness" and "That to secure these rights, Governments are instituted among Men."

Cecilia M. Kenyon, writing on the philosophy of the Declaration, has raised some questions about the logical structure of an argument

---

15. Locke, "The Second Treatise of Government," in Laslett, ed., *Two Treatises of Government*, sec. 123–124 (p. 350).

that holds that the rights enumerated in the Declaration can be secured to all men equally. With respect to the right to liberty, for example, Kenyon has inquired, "If the liberty asserted by one man should come into conflict with the liberty asserted by another, how could the rights of both men be secured? What criterion could one devise to decide which assertion of natural right was the more valid?"[16] The inconsistencies suggested by these questions are in fact specious. The rights to which Jefferson refers—and here he clearly follows Locke—are to be understood not as mandating individual or collective acts of any kind but rather as restraining men from acting in certain ways. Or, put more simply, my right to something, say my liberty, entails only prohibitions on others and not positive commands. To the extent that I am free, I am "let alone," not "forced," "required," "commanded" by others to do (or not to do) something that I "can," "am able," "have the capacity" to do. The only boundaries limiting the actions of other men are those prohibitions that extend around my liberty. Thus understood, there are no conditions under which the liberty of one man could conflict with the liberty of another, since it is perfectly consistent that neither be constrained to act (or not to act) in any noninvasive way. It follows that all voluntary arrangements are consistent with the liberty of all men.

Nor is there any substance to Kenyon's charge that "the three rights [enumerated in the Declaration] can sometimes be in conflict with each other," since each of these rights has as its basis a similar

---

16. Cecilia M. Kenyon, "The Declaration of Independence," in *Fundamental Testaments of the American Revolution* [Papers Presented Before the Second Symposium, May 10 and 11, 1973] (Washington, D.C.: Library of Congress, 1973): 37. The notion that rights are almost invariably in conflict arises when one includes in an enumeration of rights those that impose obligations on others and afflicts most contemporary discussions of the subject. This is in large part due to the fact that politicians and others who have vulgarized the language of political theory have found it to their ideological advantage to encourage the view that such conflicts are an invariable part of political life. For once it is conceded that rights, of necessity, compete, there can be only one referee, and that is the modern democratic state.

negative conception, prohibiting both public and private interference with men's actions. Thus, Kenyon's claim that "happiness as an individual right was new, and it seems even more amenable to subjective interpretation than either liberty or life"[17] completely misconstrues the nature of rights as Jefferson understood them. We would do well to emphasize that Jefferson did not claim that men had a "right to happiness" but that they had an inalienable right to pursue it. While it might be the case that one man's happiness conflicts with the happiness of another, it by no means follows that one's right—properly understood—to pursue happiness involves trespassing upon the same right in others. To affirm an inalienable right of all men to pursue their own happiness free from the interference of others is to assert no less objective a right than the right to one's life. The right to one's life does not entail that one will be free from fatal microorganisms nor that it is incumbent on others to do all they can to prevent one from dying, but only that they not actively intervene to kill you. Even under circumstances where two people are confronted with conditions such that one man's life is contingent on the other's death, neither may raise his hand against the other under pain of violating this right, despite the fact that both will die.

That Jefferson understood the rights he enumerated as impelling others, either individually or collectively, to positive actions lies at the root of a whole series of misinterpretations of the meaning of the Declaration long preceding the appearance of Kenyon's article. Thus, much has been made by certain commentators of the fact that Jefferson affirmed a right to pursue happiness rather than the more customary right to property, which Locke and the other Whig radicals had made central to their theory of inalienable rights. Gilbert Chinard, for example, viewed Jefferson's choice of language as asserting a "new principle of government," one that placed a positive obligation on the civil magistrate to ensure the happiness of his

17. Kenyon, "Declaration of Independence," 37.

subjects. "I do not believe," Chinard wrote, "that any other State paper in any nation had ever proclaimed so emphatically and with such finality that one of the essential functions of government is to make men happy."[18]

Arthur M. Schlesinger later offered a similar interpretation of Jefferson's use of "the pursuit of happiness," basing his argument on references in the revolutionary literature (particularly John Adams's *Thoughts on Government*[19]) to the notion that the happiness of the subjects is the end of government. "In short," Schlesinger concluded, "none of these spokesmen of the American cause thought of happiness as something a people were entitled simply to strive for but as something that was theirs by natural right."[20] Charles M. Wiltse, following Chinard and Schlesinger, translates Jefferson's substitution similarly. "The happiness principle," he writes, "is undoubtedly the most significant feature of Jefferson's theory of rights, for it raises government above the mere negative function of securing the individual against the encroachments of others. By recognizing a right to the pursuit of happiness, the state is committed to aid its citizens in the constructive task of obtaining their desires, whatever they may be."[21]

The political naïveté of this view of rights and government is

18. Gilbert Chinard, *Thomas Jefferson: The Apostle of Americanism* (Boston: Little, Brown and Company, 1929): 75.

19. Adams there maintained that "the happiness of society is the end of government." John Adams, *Thoughts on Government: Applicable to the Present State of the American Colonies: In a Letter from a Gentleman to His Friend* (Philadelphia: Printed for John Dunlap, 1776), quoted in Charles Francis Adams, *Works of John Adams*, IV, 193.

20. Arthur M. Schlesinger, "The Lost Meaning of 'The Pursuit of Happiness,'" *William and Mary Quarterly*, 3rd Series, XXI (1964): 326. Schlesinger offers no evidence for this conclusion nor does it follow from the four examples he offers. Indeed, the essay is so slight—it barely runs to two and a half pages—that one is tempted to conclude that it would not have seen print, at least not in this form, were it not for the reputation of its author.

21. Charles M. Wiltse, *The Jeffersonian Tradition in American Democracy* (Chapel Hill: University of North Carolina Press, 1935): 70–71.

nothing short of breathtaking. If we cannot fulfill our desires without the "constructive aid" of others, that aid can only take the form of resources that we lack. But the resources necessary to aid us in fulfilling our desires can come only from others who currently possess those resources. We are thus confronted with a situation where we are all entitled by right to more resources than exist and to a state that has no limits in determining who will attain happiness and who will not.

In so representing the thrust of the Declaration's argument, Chinard, Schlesinger, and Wiltse, among others, have failed to grasp the nature of the rights to which Jefferson refers. The Declaration describes these rights as belonging to all men by virtue of their being men, and they unmistakably precede the establishment of any political authority. Therefore, the conditions under which these rights may be exercised cannot be contingent on the actions of government; they cannot be understood as imposing a set of positive commands on others. Radical natural-law theorists, and especially Locke, whose work formed the basis of the political philosophy contained in the Declaration, held that the ends of civil government limited the extent of political authority. When men consented to the creation of that authority, they transferred only those original rights as were necessary to achieve those specific ends. A right that is inalienable cannot be so transferred, and it is among these rights that Jefferson includes "the pursuit of happiness." Not only does the right to pursue happiness, then, owe its existence to a source higher than that of any government, but also its exercise must in some crucial sense be separable and distinct from any action of government.

Much confusion surrounding what Jefferson meant when he coupled the notion of happiness with his theory of rights could be avoided if careful attention were paid to the Declaration's language. The functions of governments are clearly stipulated. Although the origins of civil authority lie in the welfare of its subjects, its duties are circumscribed to that consonant with the purposes for which it was created—namely, the securing of those inalienable rights that all men possess. The end of government is neither to maximize happiness nor to ensure that men attain happiness but to provide the framework in which each person may pursue his own happiness as he individually sees fit. To endow the term "pursuit of happiness" with tortured meanings—as Schlesinger does when he suggests that it be understood to signify the "practice" of happiness, as in the "pursuit" of law[22]—does an injustice to Jefferson's skill as a lucid prose stylist. Nor does it contravene the Declaration's assertion that the pursuit of happiness is a personal right. It is no less a distortion of the philosophy underlying the Declaration to claim that when Jefferson stipulated a right to pursue happiness, his purpose was that of asserting a scientific law, that all men cannot help but pursue happiness. The inclusion of this phrase in the Declaration, Garry Wills has claimed, reflects Jefferson's intention "to state scientific law in the human area—natural *law* as human *right*."[23] Not only is this reading incompatible with Wills's erroneous conclusion that the document "makes happiness a hard political test of any reign's very legitimacy," but it totally perverts the logical structure of the Declaration.

We must still confront the question of why Jefferson chose to employ the term "pursuit of happiness" in his list of inalienable rights instead of the more usual "property." It is almost certainly the case that Jefferson was familiar with—and possibly had before him—a copy of George Mason's Virginia Declaration of Rights when he composed the Declaration of Independence.[24] Julian Boyd notes that

22. Schlesinger, "The Lost Meaning of 'The Pursuit of Happiness,'" 325.
23. Wills, *Inventing America*: 247.
24. Pauline Maier is unequivocal on this score. "Jefferson—perhaps with some help from Franklin—made the same kind of careful editorial adjustments in the opening lines [of the preamble], which, as an examination of successive drafts of the document reveals, were based upon the first three provisions of the Mason/committee draft of Virginia's Declaration of Rights." Pauline Maier, *American Scrip-*

Mason's draft was reprinted in the *Pennsylvania Evening Post* of 6
June and again in the *Pennsylvania Gazette* of 12 June, the day
following Jefferson's appointment to a congressional committee
whose function it was to compose a declaration justifying independence.[25] The similarities between the two documents strongly suggest that Jefferson's formulation of the Declaration's preamble owed
much to Mason's document and particularly to its opening paragraph.
Mason wrote:

> All men are born equally free and independent, and have certain
> inherent Rights, of which they cannot, by any Compact, deprive or
> divest their Posterity; among which are the Enjoyment of Life and
> Liberty, with the Means of acquiring and possessing Property, and
> pursuing and obtaining Happiness and Safety.[26]

---

ture: Making the Declaration of Independence (New York: Alfred A. Knopf, 1997):
133.

25. Julian P. Boyd, *The Declaration of Independence: The Evolution of the Text*,
rev. ed. (Washington, D.C.: Library of Congress, 1999): 24.

26. George Mason, "First Draft of the Virginia Declaration of Rights," Robert A.
Rutland, ed., 3 vols. (Chapel Hill: University of North Carolina Press, 1970): I, 277.
John Adams noted, in a *Diary* entry made in 1779, that the Pennsylvania Declaration
of Rights, adopted shortly after the Virginia Convention took action on Mason's
draft, was "taken almost verbatim from that of Virginia." Article One of the Pennsylvania Declaration reads:

> That all men are born equally free and independent, and have certain
> natural, inherent and inalienable rights, amongst which are, the enjoying and
> defending life and liberty, acquiring, possessing and protecting property and
> pursuing and obtaining happiness and safety.

Compare Article One of the Massachusetts Declaration of Rights, drafted by John
Adams and adopted by the Massachusetts Constitutional Convention in 1780:

> All men are born free and equal, and have certain natural, essential, and
> unalienable rights; among which may be reckoned the right of enjoying and
> defending their lives and liberties; that of acquiring, possessing, and protecting
> property; in fine, that of seeking and obtaining their safety and happiness.

"The Pennsylvania Declaration of Rights, 1776," and "The Massachusetts
Declaration of Rights, 1780," in Bernard Schwartz, ed., *The Roots of the Bill
of Rights*, 5 vols. (New York: Chelsea House Publishers, 1980): II: 264, 340.

It seems probable that Jefferson, who was as familiar with this view of inherent rights as was Mason and who espoused it with no less fervor, decided to compress the notion of a right comprising "the Means of acquiring and possessing Property, and pursuing and obtaining Happiness and Safety" into a more concise right to pursue happiness. The right to pursue one's happiness does not, nor was it meant to, preclude the right to acquire, maintain, or transfer property, which—in any of its specific forms—is alienable by consent.[27] When Jefferson wrote of an inalienable right to the pursuit of happiness, he was asserting a broader right that guaranteed to all men the freedom both to choose the form their own happiness would take and to seek to attain that happiness as they saw fit. The right to pursue one's happiness is inclusive of a natural right to the products of one's labor, just as the right to pursue the means to certain ends is implied by a right to pursue those ends. By substituting the words "pursuit of happiness," Jefferson was in no way disavowing a natural right to property, as Locke and the other Whig theorists understood the term.

Certain critics, antagonistic to the concept of property rights, have insisted on reading into Jefferson's words an outright rejection of the notion of private property as an indefeasible right. Thus, Vernon L.

27. The distinction between an inalienable right to property and the fact that specific property can be alienated appears to have caused hopeless confusion in Wills's analysis of the Declaration and in that of Allen Jayne (*Jefferson's Declaration of Independence: Origins, Philosophy, and Theology* (Lexington: University Press of Kentucky, 1998)). Jayne uses the fact that, since Henry Home, Lord Kames had clearly shown that it is possible "to alienate property in the form of movable goods and land," and inasmuch as Kames's work was well known to Jefferson, Jefferson was forced to substitute an inalienable right to pursue happiness for an inalienable right to property. Indeed, according to Jayne, the change further reflects the substantial influence Kames had on shaping Jefferson's political thinking (Jayne, *Jefferson's Declaration of Independence*, 120–26). Both Wills and Jayne suffer from the common error of reading the Declaration of Independence as if it were an essay in moral philosophy rather than a document of political principles. The two are related, but they are by no means identical.

Parrington concluded that "the substitution of 'pursuit of happiness' for 'property' marks a complete break with the Whiggish doctrine of property rights that Locke bequeathed to the English middle class, and the substitution that gave to the document the note of idealism which was to make its appeal so perennially human and vital."[28] That Parrington did not find the concept of a right to property "human and vital," however, is not to suggest that it was not so regarded by Jefferson and the other patriots caught up in the revolutionary struggle. Jefferson's own views on the question are plainly set forth in a letter to Dupont de Nemours in 1816, in which he wrote that "a right to property is founded on our natural wants, in the means with which we are endowed to satisfy these wants, and the right to what we acquire by those means without violating the similar rights of other sensible beings."[29] And, with respect to the relation between government and the individual's right to liberty and to the product of his labors, Jefferson remarked in his first inaugural address:

> Still one thing more, fellow citizens—a wise and frugal government, which shall restrain men from injuring one another, which shall leave them otherwise to regulate their own pursuits of industry and improvement, and shall not take from the month of labor the bread it has earned. This is the sum of good government, and this is necessary to close the circle of our felicities.[30]

This sentiment epitomizes the philosophy that Jefferson had affirmed in the Declaration. Although the document's preamble underwent a series of changes between the time Jefferson completed

28. Vernon L. Parrington, *Main Currents in American Thought*, vol. I, *1620–1800: The Colonial Mind* (Harvest Books; New York: Harcourt, Brace, Jovanovich, 1954): 350.

29. Jefferson to Pierre Samuel Dupont de Nemours, 24 April 1816, Andrew A. Lipscomb and Albert Ellery Bergh, eds., *The Writings of Thomas Jefferson*, 20 vols. (Washington, D.C.: Thomas Jefferson Memorial Association, 1903–1905): XIV: 490.

30. Jefferson, "First Inaugural Address" [4 March 1801], *Writings* (Library of America; New York: Literary Classics of the United States, 1983): 494.

his original draft—before he submitted it to the other members of the drafting committee—and its final adoption by Congress, nothing of critical philosophical importance was altered. Carl L. Becker has succeeded in reconstructing Jefferson's basic text by comparing his Rough Draft, which contains a whole series of corrections and emendations made at all stages of the document's evolution, with copies of the Declaration as it read at several points before its final adoption. The critical portion of the preamble, as Jefferson originally wrote it, reads

> We hold these truths to be sacred & undeniable; that all men are created equal and independent, that from that equal creation they derive rights inherent and inalienable, among which are the preservation of life, & liberty, & the pursuit of happiness; that to secure these ends, governments are instituted among men, deriving their just powers from the consent of the governed; that whenever any form of government shall become destructive of these ends, it is the right of the people to alter or abolish it, & to institute new government, laying it's foundations on such principles & organizing it's powers in such form, as to them shall seem most likely to effect their safety & happiness.[31]

With reference to Jefferson's original wording, Morton White argues that the change from "ends" to "rights" in the document's clause respecting what it is that governments are to secure ("the preservation of life, & liberty, & the pursuit of happiness") marks a fundamental philosophical shift in the Declaration's statement concerning the purpose of government.[32] In the context here used, White contended, Jefferson could have meant only that the functions of government were more positive and far-reaching than those narrowly consistent

31. The draft is printed in Carl L. Becker, *The Declaration of Independence: A Study in the History of Political Ideas* (New York: Random House, 1922): 142. A holographic version of this draft appears in Boyd, *Declaration of Independence*, 67–71.

32. Morton White, *The Philosophy of the American Revolution* (New York: Oxford University Press, 1978): 244–56.

with the preservation of natural rights. White's analysis rests on interpreting the word "secure" in "secure these ends" to mean "attain" rather than "guard." White acknowledges that the change in wording, from "ends" to "rights," was made by Jefferson himself before the document was submitted to Congress for its consideration. But in doing so, White concludes, Jefferson altered the Declaration's political philosophy "so as to give the impression that governments are instituted to *secure* in the sense of *guard* certain *rights* rather than that they are instituted to *secure* in the sense of *attain* certain *ends*." This change, White suggests, reflected Jefferson's ambiguity respecting "whether the end of government is merely to protect certain rights or whether government was to go further and *encourage* man's exercise of those rights."[33]

As interesting as White's analysis is, there are several problems with accepting his conclusion that when Jefferson drafted the Declaration "two warring philosophical souls dwelt within [his] breast."[34] Jefferson himself appears to have regarded the changes made in the draft before its submission to Congress as of minor importance only; in writing of these alterations to James Madison some years later, he referred to them as "merely verbal."[35] Indeed, there is no evidence

33. White, *Philosophy of the American Revolution*, 255, 252.

34. White, *Philosophy of the American Revolution*, 255.

35. Jefferson to James Madison, 30 August 1823, in Ford, ed., *Writings*, 269. Jefferson's letter to Madison was written in response to charges by John Adams that the ideas and language of the Declaration were far from new. Adams had written Timothy Pickering some years after the Declaration had been adopted, pointing out its lack of originality. "As you justly observe," he notes, "there is not an idea in it, but what had been hackney'd in Congress for two years before. The substance of it is contained in the Declaration of rights and the violation of those rights, in the Journal of Congress in 1774. Indeed, the essence of it is contained in a pamphlet, voted and printed by the Town of Boston before the first Congress met, composed by James Otis, as I suppose—in one of his lucid intervals, and pruned and polished by Sam Adams." (Adams to Timothy Pickering, 6 August 1822, in Charles Francis Adams, ed., *The Works of John Adams*, II: 514). At the Fourth of July celebrations at Salem, Massachusetts, in 1823, Pickering quoted from Adams's letter deprecating Jefferson's contributions, to which Jefferson felt obligated to respond, which he did in a

that Jefferson perceived that there was any important philosophical difference between his original reference to "ends" and his subsequent use of "rights." Nor is there any compelling reason to accept White's inference that when Jefferson wrote "to secure these ends" he meant this term to signify that the function of government was to actively "aid and abet men in attaining ends proposed by God."[36] In fact, when Jefferson asserted that governments are instituted among men to secure these ends, namely, the preservation of life and liberty and the pursuit of happiness, he probably meant no more than did Locke, who announced in *The Second Treatise* that the great end of men's putting themselves under government is the preservation of their lives, liberties, and estates.

The change from "ends" to "rights" was not the only revision that either Jefferson or the other members of the drafting committee made to the basic text before the document was reported to Congress on 28 June. Boyd has calculated that the Rough Draft, as finally submitted, contained forty-seven alterations. Some of these were of no importance, such as the deletion of a partially written word, while others were made for what appear to be purely stylistic purposes. In addition, Jefferson supplemented his bill of indictment against the Crown by appending three new charges. Of these revisions and additions, only seven are apparently in a hand other than Jefferson's; two would seem to have been made by Adams, and the others by

---

letter to James Madison. The letter in part reads: "Pickering's observations, and Mr. Adam's in addition, 'that it contained no new ideas, that it is a common place compilation, it's sentiments hacknied in Congress for two years before, and it's essence contained in Otis's pamphlet' may all be true. Of that I am not the judge. Richard H. Lee charged it as copied from Locke's treatise on government. Otis's pamphlet I never saw & whether I had gathered my ideas from reading or reflection I do not know. I know only that I turned to neither book or pamphlet while writing it. I did not consider it as any part of my charge to invent new ideas altogether & to offer no sentiment which had ever been expressed before." Jefferson to James Madison, 30 August 1823, in Ford, ed., *Writings*, 269.

36. White, *Philosophy of the American Revolution*, 255.

Franklin. It appears probable that all the changes occurring in the Declaration's philosophical preamble as reported to Congress were Jefferson's.

This discussion of rights and the Declaration need not linger on the list of grievances, which constitutes the major portion of the Declaration. It should be noted, however, that the charges specified in the document were leveled not against the Parliament of Great Britain, but against the Crown. The American conception of the constitutional status of the colonies within the British empire viewed them as linked to Great Britain only in the sense that they acknowledged a common monarch.[37] The Parliament of Great Britain had no more legal authority over the various provinces of British North America than the House of Burgesses of Virginia had over Great Britain or over any other dominion owing allegiance to George III. By mid-1776, this view had become commonplace among Americans. They regarded their fealty to the King as one that had originally been assumed voluntarily—that is, by the consent of the people—and they thus felt free to retract it at their pleasure. The colonists' right to rebel against tyrannical government was predicated not only on the privileges that they possessed as British subjects but also on the natural rights that they, in company with all men at all times, possessed. And the injuries and usurpations under which the colonists suffered, as enumerated in the Declaration's indictment, were not simply trespasses on the privileges traditionally accorded Englishmen by their sovereign but also violations of the colonists' fundamental indefeasible rights as human beings. This view was adumbrated in Jefferson's A Summary View of the Rights of British America in 1774, and in his draft of the Declaration of the Causes and Necessity of Taking Up Arms, composed at the beginning of July 1775.

There is a body of scholarly opinion that minimizes the centrality

37. And that at the colony's inception they shared a common body of laws and privileges, since it was a juridical given that "the law follows the flag."

and importance of the Declaration and contends that the claims
made by the American colonists in their controversies with Great
Britain were consistently framed in the language of English rights
and that arguments based on the authority of natural law were irrel-
evant to the debate. For example, one of the most prolific legal
historians of the period, John Philip Reid,[38] claims unequivocally that
"the revolutionary controversy was concerned with positive constitutional rights, not abstract natural rights," and that "at every important occasion when the American whig leadership gathered to claim
rights and state grievances, nature was rejected as the sole authority
for rights."[39] But even Reid's somewhat extravagant assertions con-
cede that the colonists did in fact often appeal to the law of nature
as an alternative authority for the rights they asserted. Nor does there
seem much doubt, despite Reid's reservations, that, as open rebellion
with Great Britain approached, the colonists increasingly resorted to
arguments based not on the prerogatives peculiar to Englishmen but
rather on man's natural rights. Indeed, Reid himself offers several
examples in which the colonial position is couched in terms that are
unambiguously grounded on the law of nature. Thus, among the
resolutions of the freeholders of Granville County in 1774 is the
following: "Resolved. That those absolute rights we are entitled to as
men, by the immutable Laws of Nature, are antecedent to all social
and relative duties whatsoever." Similarly, the Boston Declaration
of 1772, which invokes the "eternal and immutable Laws of God
and nature" and whose introductory comments read like a précis of
Locke's *Treatises of Government*, provides that "among the natural

---

38. See John Philip Reid's four-volume study, *Constitutional History of the Amer-
ican Revolution*, vol. I, *The Authority of Rights* (Madison: University of Wisconsin
Press, 1986); vol. II, *The Authority to Tax* (Madison: University of Wisconsin Press,
1987); vol. III, *The Authority to Legislate* (Madison: University of Wisconsin
Press, 1991); and vol. IV, *The Authority of Law* (Madison: University of Wisconsin
Press, 1993).

39. John Philip Reid, *Constitutional History of the American Revolution*, vol. I,
The Authority of Rights, 90, 91.

rights of the colonists are these; first, a right to life; secondly, to liberty; thirdly, to property; together with the right to support and defend them in the best manner they can."[40] And, with particular reference to the protections afforded Americans by the several colonial charters, James Otis observed: "Should the charter privileges of the Colonists be disregarded or revoked, there are natural, inherent, and inseparable rights as men and citizens that would remain."[41]

Finally, the language of the Declaration of Independence would seem to offer overwhelming evidence of the pervasiveness of the Lockean notion of rights among the colonists. There is no reason to question Jefferson's claim, when writing some years later about the political principles contained in the Declaration, that, "with respect to our rights, and the acts of the British government contravening those rights, there was but one opinion on this side of the water; all American whigs thought alike on these subjects."[42] As we have seen, the truth of Jefferson's assertion is vouchsafed by the fact that several states, as part of their new constitutions, enacted declarations of rights explicitly couched in Lockean language by the end of 1776, particularly Virginia and Pennsylvania.[43]

40. "The Rights of the Colonists and a List of Infringements and Violations of Rights, 1772," in Bernard Schwartz, ed., *The Roots of the Bill of Rights*, I: 200–11.

41. James Otis, *The Rights of the British Colonies Asserted and Proved* (Boston: Printed and Sold by Edes and Gill, 1764).

42. Jefferson to Henry Lee, 8 May 1825, in Ford, ed., *The Writings of Thomas Jefferson*, X: 343.

43. Much has been made of the absence of any theoretical preamble to many of the colonial charters that were drafted in the early history of British North America and the fact that the protections that these charters afforded were regularly couched in terms of the traditional prerogatives accorded Englishmen rather than reflecting a conception of rights derivable from nature. According to Reid, the Continental Congress's Declaration of Independence was in this respect idiosyncratic. But this is to mistake the purpose of these charters, which was to provide a frame of government for each of the colonies. To the extent that they set limits to the powers of the colonial governments, it is to be expected that these constitutional charters would concern themselves primarily with the procedural protections accorded the colonists as Englishmen living overseas. Even the Fundamental Constitution of Carolina,

I have already indicated that the constraints of space prevent detailed discussion of the grievances contained in the Declaration. However, some mention must be made of certain charges in Jefferson's bill of indictment. Sometime in late May or early June 1776 Jefferson had written a draft of a proposed constitution for Virginia, the preamble to which enumerated a series of injuries suffered by the colonies at the hands of the British Crown. The basic text of the Declaration contains eighteen grievances, one of which is divided into eight distinct counts, making twenty-five charges in all. Of these, twenty were taken almost verbatim from the earlier document and, with two exceptions, appear in the same order. The sequence and language of the charges enumerated in the Declaration, Boyd observed, appear to leave no question that Jefferson had the text of his Preamble to the Virginia Constitution before him when he composed the grievances incorporated in the document.[44]

Before submitting the draft of the Declaration to Congress, Jefferson added three new charges against George III, among them a

_____

which provides that "no person whatsoever shall disturb, molest, or persecute another for his speculative opinions in religion, or his way of worship," ("The Fundamental Constitution of Carolina, 1669," in Bernard Schwartz, ed., *Roots of the Bill of Rights*, I: 123) a protection that goes far beyond any then existing in England, does not suggest whence this right derives. It is only because its author is John Locke that we know that its source is in the law of nature itself. Indeed, many of the protections mentioned in the various charters at the least suggest that they are included by virtue of the colonists' humanity and were derived from God or nature, and not from the state. Even with respect to the provisions that dealt with the specific powers granted the various colonial governments, it is apparent that the rights that were subject to legislative construction, such as the right to property, could be circumscribed only under the strictest conditions. Thus, the Massachusetts Body of Liberties specified that "no mans goods or estaite shall be taken away from him, nor any way indammaged under coulor of law or Countenance of Authoritie, unless it be by virtue or equitie of some expresse law of the Country waranting the same, established by a generall Court and sufficiently published, or in case of the defect of a law in any particular case by the word of god" ("Massachusetts Body of Liberties, 1641," in Bernard Schwartz, ed., *Roots of the Bill of Rights*, I: 72).

44. Boyd, *Declaration of Independence*, 22.

censure of the Quebec Act of 1774, which extended the boundaries of Quebec to the Mississippi River in the west and southward to the Ohio River. The act further provided that legislative authority in the province be vested solely in a royally appointed council and granted to the British Parliament the power to levy all but purely local taxes. Finally, English civil law was abolished and the Anglican church disestablished. In their place, French civil law, which precluded the trial of civil cases by jury, was reinstituted, and Roman Catholicism was reimposed as the established communion, one section of the bill expressly guaranteeing to the clergy the "dues and rights" they had earlier received under the French regime. This pernicious act, restoring many of the laws and religious privileges earlier imposed by an openly autocratic regime on a territory that would henceforth constitute the largest area of North America, was regarded with particular loathing by the colonists, who saw in it a direct threat to their own political and civil institutions.

By far the most significant addition to Jefferson's charges was his denunciation of slavery. At some point between the completion of his original text and submission of the draft of the Declaration to Congress, Jefferson added the following indictment of George III:

> He has waged cruel war against human nature itself, violating its most sacred rights of life and liberty in the persons of a distant people who never offended him, captivating and carrying them into slavery in another hemisphere, or to incur miserable death in their transportation thither. This piratical warfare, the opprobrium of *infidel* powers, is the warfare of the *Christian* king of Great Britain. Determined to keep open a market where MEN should be bought and sold, he has prostituted his negative for suppressing every legislative attempt to prohibit or to restrain this execrable commerce.

Becker, among others, has suggested that there was something hypocritical in the charge, which, like the others, is couched in the form of an indictment of the Crown.[45] Certainly it is true that the subsequent history of the slave trade and of slavery itself in the United States points to more villainy on this side of the Atlantic than in Great Britain. But there is a complex of irrefragable evidence pointing to the complicity of the British government in perpetuating this satanic institution. Edward Dumbauld notes that on at least six occasions colonial acts imposing prohibitively high duties on the slave trade were disallowed by the king-in-council, thus permitting an unusually lucrative British market to flourish unhindered.[46] Of far greater importance, however, is the fact that a document proclaiming the inalienable natural rights of all men—and this probably accounts for why "men" is capitalized in Jefferson's draft—should have vigorously condemned slavery as inimical to the principles upon which the new nation was to rest. The excision of this charge by Congress cannot but have impoverished the document, just as the institution itself was to impoverish the republic until its bloody repudiation ninety years later.

On 28 June Jefferson and the other members of the committee reported the amended draft of the Declaration to Congress. Jefferson is known to have consulted with Adams and Franklin, both of whom had made minor revisions to the language of the document, after

45. Becker, *Declaration of Independence*, 213.

46. "[There had been] numerous occasions when attempts by the Colonies to abolish the slave trade had been repeatedly 'defeated by his majesty's negative.' Imposition of prohibitive duties on the importation of slaves ran counter to the King's policy of protecting a profitable British trade from legislative interference. Though the Virginia House of Burgesses, on April 1, 1772, petitioned the King to permit the Governor to assent to laws which would 'check so very pernicious a Commerce,' the British government refused to relax its instructions. These forbade laws detrimental to British commercial interests, and specifically commanded 'that no Duty be laid on any Slave Imported payable by the Importer.' The Virginia law of April 11, 1772, was disallowed in England, just as earlier efforts to curb the slave trade, made by Virginia and by other colonies, had met the same fate." Dumbauld, *Declaration of Independence*, 89.

which the draft was submitted to the whole committee. There is, unfortunately, no way to determine whether any of the alterations and additions that appear in Jefferson's own handwriting were the result of suggestions made by the other members or were the product of Jefferson's own judgment; nor, indeed, is it possible to determine whether these changes were made before or after Sherman and Livingston were first shown Jefferson's draft. Given the style of the revisions and Jefferson's later recounting of the events of this period, it is not unlikely that at least the greater part of the emendations made in the basic text were Jefferson's alone.

On 2 July the Congress, at the outset meeting in Committee of the Whole, adopted the Lee resolution, whereby the American colonies declared themselves to be free and independent states, absolved from all allegiance to the British Crown. The vote on the resolution would have been unanimous if the New York delegation had not felt compelled to abstain, having received no reply from the provincial congress to their earlier request for instructions. On 1 July a preliminary vote showed only nine colonies prepared to support independence. Both South Carolina and Pennsylvania voted against the Lee resolution, New York abstained, and the two delegates from Delaware then present in Philadelphia were divided on the issue. By the next day, however, a dramatic shift had occurred. The South Carolina delegation, led by Edward Rutledge, joined the pro-independence faction for the sake of intercolonial unity, and the Delaware delegation was enlarged by the last-minute arrival of Caesar Rodney, hastily called from Dover to cast that colony's tie-breaking vote in favor of independence. Finally, Pennsylvania's delegation, which had opposed the Lee resolution by a vote of four to three on 1 July, moved into the independence camp when two opponents, John Dickinson and Robert Morris, deliberately absented themselves on the following day. Thus, on 2 July, with twelve delegations voting in favor and one abstaining, the united colonies declared their independence from Great Britain and so became free states.

Following passage of the Lee resolution, the Congress immediately turned its attention to consideration of the Declaration, whose function was to justify the decision just reached. Inasmuch as the debate on the Declaration was undertaken by Congress again meeting in Committee of the Whole, the Rough and Corrected Journals are silent on the nature of the discussion that took place. It is known that a number of alterations and deletions were made, many for purely stylistic purposes. There appears to have been no attempt to tamper with the Declaration's theory of government, so eloquently expressed in Jefferson's preamble. Indeed, the view of government there affirmed was the product of legal and political principles embraced by all the revolutionaries, as it emerged in the writing of natural-rights theorists from Hugo Grotius and Samuel Pufendorf, through Locke and the other Whig radicals, to the continental writers inspired by Locke, particularly Jean Jacques Burlamaqui. Congress made only two minor changes in the phrasing of Jefferson's philosophical preamble: "inherent and unalienable rights" was altered to "certain unalienable rights," and the words "begun at a distinguished period, and" were deleted from Jefferson's more wordy "But when a long train of abuses & usurpations, begun at a distinguished period, & pursuing invariably the same Object evinces a design to reduce them under absolute Despotism."

The Congress did not stop at minor revisions, however. It excised two major passages from the draft as submitted, among them, as already noted, Jefferson's condemnation of slavery and the slave trade. The second major deletion involved Jefferson's final paragraph, in which he denounced the British electorate for its complicity in the abuses perpetrated by the British government in North America. As the author of the Declaration, Jefferson was naturally disheartened that Congress should have seen fit to use so heavy a hand in editing a document that had been framed with such care. He appears to have been particularly offended at the deletion of the paragraph on slavery and his indictment of the British public. With respect to these excisions, he observed in his notes on the proceedings of Congress:

> The pusillanimous idea that we had friends in England worth keeping terms with, still haunted the minds of many. For this reason those passages which conveyed censures on the people of England were struck out, lest they should give them offence. The clause too, reprobating the enslaving the inhabitants of Africa, was struck out in complaisance to South Carolina & Georgia, who had never attempted to restrain the importation of slaves, and who on the contrary still wished to continue it. Our Northern brethren also I believe felt a little tender under those censures; for tho' their people have very few slaves themselves yet they had been very considerable carriers of them to others.[47]

Jefferson was predictably convinced that his final draft was superior to the Declaration as Congress amended it, and he sent copies of the text as he submitted it to several friends, both while it was being altered by Congress and soon afterward. But, with the exception of its deletion of his condemnation of the slave trade, the reader is compelled to agree with Boyd that "it is difficult to point out a passage in the Declaration, great as it was, that was not improved by [Congress's] attention. That a public body would reduce rather than increase the number of words in a political document is in itself a remarkable testimony to their sagacity and ability to express themselves. Certainly the final paragraph, considered as parliamentary practice, as political principle, and as literature was greatly improved by the changes of Congress."[48]

On the evening of 4 July the Declaration, as amended, was reported by the Committee of the Whole and duly approved by the Congress without dissent. The document was then ordered authenticated and printed, at which point John Hancock signed the au-

---

47. Jefferson, "Notes of Proceedings in the Continental Congress," in *Papers of Thomas Jefferson*, vol. I, *1760–1776*, 314–15.
48. Boyd, *Declaration of Independence*, 35.

thenticated copy "by Order and in Behalf of Congress." At that moment, it is reported, the bell atop the State House, where the Congress was then meeting, began to ring to herald the event. The bell itself is inscribed with the following words from Leviticus: "Proclaim liberty throughout the land unto all the inhabitants thereof." No nation—no kingdom or principality—was born with greater majesty than was the United States, whose founding charter proclaimed to the world the revolutionary doctrine that all men, no matter how base their status, were endowed with God-given rights, upon which governments trespassed only at the gravest peril.

The conception of rights embraced by the American revolutionary theorists and reflected in the Declaration conceived of them as eternal and immutable, as antedating the establishment of all political authority, and as belonging to all men by virtue of their humanity alone. Since their exercise does not conflict with others' rights, this conception logically entails the strictest limits on the actions of government, a notion that shaped much of early American political philosophy. The gradual erosion of this understanding of rights and its replacement with the view that individual rights conflict with one another and that their exercise requires that others be impelled to act in certain ways entails a very different conception of government, one in which the political authority is required to intervene actively, both to mediate between the rights of citizens and to provide the means whereby certain rights can be realized. It is important, when examining the way rights were understood by the American revolutionaries, that this second, more modern, and somewhat vulgar conception is not confused with the way the eighteenth century understood the term, as so often happens. Fortunately, this newer notion of rights has not totally supplanted its eighteenth-century rival, which still serves to animate citizens against the arbitrary incursions of a despotic government. We all owe a great deal to seventeenth- and eighteenth-century political theory and particularly to radical Whig thought for providing a theory of rights and of government consistent with individual autonomy and freedom. While so many of the insights that the eighteenth century has furnished us have been abandoned, we still remain indebted for a conception of rights that places the individual above the state and that makes the ultimate test of government whether those rights are protected.

John Adams had expected that the new nation would commemorate 2 July, the date on which Lee's resolution of independence passed Congress, as its independence day, but through a curious anomaly 4 July received the honor. The date that Americans annually celebrate is not the anniversary of the day on which independence from Great Britain was first declared but rather the anniversary of the day on which the Congress proclaimed a universal theory of government based on the inalienable rights of man. It is altogether fitting to the American spirit that we commemorate not merely a political act but also an ideological one.

On 9 July the New York provincial congress, sitting in White Plains, voted unanimously to ratify the Declaration. On 19 July, four days after New York's acquiescence had been read to the Congress, it was ordered that the Declaration be engrossed on parchment and that its title be altered to "The Unanimous Declaration of the 13 United States of America." Finally, on 2 August the engrossed copy was signed by the members of the Continental Congress. Immediately after its passage, copies of the Declaration had been dispatched to all the colonies, where it was read with suitable pomp and celebration before approving crowds; for this charter upon which the new republic was founded gave voice to the fact that the war in which the colonists were then engaged was in reality the most principled act of rebellion against despotism of which mankind has record.

CHAPTER TWO

Saving Rights Theory from Its Friends

Tom G. Palmer

RIGHTS ARE AN INTEGRAL PART of the American experiment. They enjoy pride of place in the founding document of American independence, which famously proclaims

> that all men are created equal, that they are endowed by their creator with certain unalienable rights, that among these are life, liberty, and the pursuit of happiness; that to secure these rights, governments are instituted among men, deriving their just powers from the consent of the governed.

Perhaps because securing the mere "pursuit" of happiness does not guarantee success, or perhaps because "pursuit" seems such an elastic term, some modern interpreters of this tradition of rights believe that new rights can be and are coined by the legislature. Some seem to believe that since rights are such good things, the more of them we have, the better off we are. Hence, whenever we determine that something is good—education, housing, or the general condition of well-being we refer to as "welfare"—then legislatures should recognize rights, not merely to pursue those things, but to have them. Others have perceived that rights can be "costly," precisely because they normally imply some restriction or obligation for others, and therefore that we should coin only those rights whose benefits (to whomever) are greater than their costs. The coining of "new rights" in recent years has led to such absurdities that some have proposed a moratorium on rights talk, or even dispensing with rights talk altogether.

It has long been recognized that the subject of rights is fraught with difficulty, partly because all talk of moral obligation is difficult (the is-ought problem always raises its head) and partly because of the wide variety of existing or possible rights regimes and the difficulty of settling on just what does or does not qualify as a right. Recently to these age-old problems of moral and political philosophy have been added far more serious problems of logical coherence. As a result, it would not be too strong a statement to say that there is a crisis in rights theory.

How to straighten out the tangled knot that rights talk has become? I propose a conceptual clarification of what we mean by rights, undertaken first by means of a critique of some prominent critics of traditional rights theory and then by means of a brief excursus through the history of the concept of rights that informed the American founding. Like all concepts, discourse about rights must be guided by logic, and the use of logic may help us to arrive at a coherent and useful conception of rights. Also, like all concepts, the concept of rights has a history, and that history may help us to get straight on what rights are.

INCOHERENT RIGHTS TALK

I'll begin with a look at a work on rights by two leading legal philosophers. I do so not only because of the prominence of the work's authors but also because the problems revealed in their work are symptomatic of the current crisis in rights theory. Stephen Holmes and Cass R. Sunstein, in *The Cost of Rights: Why Liberty Depends on Taxes*, propose to achieve "enhanced clarity of focus" by considering "exclusively rights that are enforceable by politically organized communities."[1] They declare, "Under American law, rights are powers granted by the political community."[2] It's not at all clear from the text what Holmes and Sunstein mean by "American law," for all of their claims are purely conceptual and have no connection with distinctly American jurisprudence or history. In addition, of course, it flies in the face of the explicit declarations of the Declaration of Independence and the Constitution of the United States of America. But let's set that aside and turn to their philosophical arguments on behalf of the idea that rights are purely creatures of the state.

Holmes and Sunstein seek in their work to eliminate even the possibility of a conceptual distinction between "negative" rights to noninterference (the right not to be murdered, for example, or the right to free exercise of religion) and "positive" or "welfare" rights (such as the right to a subsidized education or to a house built by another person). They argue that "apparently nonwelfare rights are welfare rights too" and that "all legal rights are, or aspire to be, welfare rights."[3] Thus, they see no difference between the right to the "pursuit" of happiness and the right to happiness itself (or to a house, an education, or some other benefit); all rights are "powers granted by the political community."[4]

---

1. Stephen Holmes and Cass R. Sunstein, *The Cost of Rights: Why Liberty Depends on Taxes* (New York: W. W. Norton, 1999), p. 21. To be more precise, what Holmes and Sunstein consider are not rights that are enforce*able*, but rights that actually are enforce*d*. They combine a strong attachment to legal positivism, i.e., to the doctrine that rights are posited, with an "interest" theory of rights: "an interest qualifies as a right when an effective legal system treats it as such by using collective resources to defend it." (17) For a comparison of "interest" theories and "choice" theories of rights, see Matthew H. Kramer, Nigel Simmonds, and Hillel Steiner, *A Debate over Rights: Philosophical Enquiries* (Oxford: Clarendon Press, 1998). For the working out of the different approaches in courts of law, see John Hasnas, "From Cannibalism to Caesareans: Two Conceptions of Fundamental Rights," *Northwestern University Law Review*, 89:3 (Spring 1995), pp. 900–41.

2. Holmes and Sunstein, p. 17.

3. Holmes and Sunstein, pp. 219, 222.

4. Nowhere do Holmes and Sunstein justify this remarkable claim about the character of rights under "American law." Indeed, it would be a very difficult task to

Holmes and Sunstein identify the traditional view of rights with "opposition to government," which would be a confusion, for, as they note, "individual rights and freedoms depend fundamentally on vigorous state action."[5] More radically, "Statelessness spells rightslessness."[6] But what they intend by the term "depend fundamentally" is not

> that to secure these rights, governments are instituted among men, deriving their just powers from the consent of the governed; that whenever any form of government becomes destructive of these ends, it is the right of the people to alter or to abolish it, and to institute new government, laying its foundation on such principles, and organizing its powers in such form, as to them shall seem most likely to effect their safety and happiness.

Nor do they seem to mean that

> We the people of the United States, in order to form a more perfect union, establish justice, insure domestic tranquility, provide for the common defense, promote the general welfare, and secure the blessings of liberty to ourselves and our posterity, do ordain and establish this Constitution for the United States of America.

Under the traditional conception, the people are endowed with rights, some of which (the execution of their natural rights) they give up in order to enter civil society and which they then transfer to a government in order to defend those rights they have "retained." But, apparently finding this approach incompatible with their own philosophical orientation or agenda, Holmes and Sunstein assert as a

---

reconcile such a claim with the Ninth Amendment to the Constitution: "The enumeration in the Constitution of certain rights shall not be construed to deny or disparage others retained by the people." The language is quite clear: Just because some rights are enumerated does not mean that those are all there are. Indeed, the unenumerated rights are "retained" by the people, which means that they must preexist the establishment of government; otherwise, they could not be "retained."

5. Ibid., pp. 13, 14.
6. Ibid., p. 19.

truism that government creates rights *ex nihilo* and that this is a matter of "American law." These authors brush aside discussion of moral rights and consider only legal rights—those rights that a state will actually enforce—on the ground that "When they are not backed by legal force, by contrast, moral rights are toothless by definition. Unenforced moral rights are aspirations binding on conscience, not powers binding on officials."[7]

A careful look at the theory advanced by Holmes and Sunstein will go far in showing the profound conceptual and logical problems inherent in attempts to replace the traditional approach to rights articulated by and embodied in the Declaration of Independence and the United States Constitution.

Holmes and Sunstein ground their attempt to erase the distinction between negative and positive rights on a commonsense observation: All choices have costs. That is a conceptual or analytical claim, for to choose X over Y is to give up Y, which (if it is the most highly valued alternative forgone) is defined as the cost of choosing X. This is unobjectionable, thus far. They proceed to note that the act of choosing to enforce a right, like all choices, has a cost—namely, the most highly valued opportunity forgone. Combining that insight with the claim that the only rights that are meaningful are those that are actually enforced, they conclude that since the enforcement of rights has costs, rights themselves have costs. Thus the subtitle to the book: *Why Liberty Depends on Taxes.* All acts of enforcement have costs and require the mobilization of resources—police, judges, jailers, executioners, and so on—and are therefore positive claims on the expenditure of taxes (or other forms of compulsion; conscription would fill the bill as well as taxation) to secure those resources. The right not to be killed is thereby converted into the right to police protection, which entails the expenditure of resources and therefore choices among alternative uses of those resources. Thus, the allegedly

7. Ibid., p. 17.

"negative" right not to be killed is indistinguishable from the "positive" right to the expenditure of resources to hire or conscript police.

According to Holmes and Sunstein,

> Rights are costly because remedies are costly. Enforcement is expensive, especially uniform and fair enforcement; and legal rights are hollow to the extent that they remain unenforced. Formulated differently, almost every right implies a correlative duty, and duties are taken seriously only when dereliction is punished by the public power drawing on the public purse.[8]

Even "the right against being tortured by police officers and prison guards" is, contrary to traditional thinking, not a negative right against interference but a positive right to have monitors hired by the state to supervise the police officers and prison guards:

> A state that cannot arrange prompt visits to jails and prisons by taxpayer-salaried doctors, prepared to submit credible evidence at trial, cannot effectively protect the incarcerated against torture and beatings. All rights are costly because all rights presuppose taxpayer-funding of effective supervisory machinery for monitoring and enforcement.[9]

Here their theory begins to run into very serious logical difficulties, for the account of rights and obligations on which they base that theory generates an infinite regress.

Holmes and Sunstein argue that I cannot have a right not to be tortured by the police unless the police have an obligation not to

---

8. Ibid., p. 43. Thus, Holmes and Sunstein incorporate a principle of positive social theory into their normative account of rights, namely, that order obtains *only* when a sovereign power threatens punishment. This is hardly a self-evident claim, but it is clearly an important element of their assault on the traditional view of rights. Traditional rights theory is normally complemented by a theory of "spontaneous order," according to which order need not be the result of an ordering authority with power to punish deviations from its imposed order. That does not mean that punishment is never needed, but that the ever-present threat of punishment is not the only or even the primary force in creating social order.

9. Ibid., p. 44.

torture me, and the police can only have an obligation not to torture me if there are some taxpayer-funded persons (monitors) above the police who can punish them (since "duties are taken seriously only when dereliction is punished by the public power drawing on the public purse"). So to have a right not to be tortured by the police, I would have to have a right that the monitors exercise their power to punish the police in the event that the police torture me. But do I have a right that the monitors exercise their power to punish the police for torturing me? According to Holmes and Sunstein, I would have such a right only if the monitors had a duty to punish the police, and the monitors would have a duty to punish the police only if there were some taxpayer-funded persons above the monitors who could (and would) punish the monitors for failing to punish the police, and so on, *ad infinitum*. For there ever to be a right of any sort, by their own reasoning, there would have to be an infinite hierarchy of people threatening to punish those lower in the hierarchy. Since there is no infinite hierarchy, we are forced to conclude that Holmes and Sunstein have actually offered an impossibility theorem of rights in the logical form of *modus tollens*: If there are rights, then there must be an infinite hierarchy of power; there is not an infinite hierarchy of power, therefore there are no rights.

In working out their theory, Holmes and Sunstein generate not "clarity of focus" but logical chaos and incoherence.

The theory of liberty that Holmes and Sunstein advance also leads to strange conclusions. Holmes and Sunstein use the terms "rights" and "liberty" interchangeably, not only in the title of the book but also in the text.[10] Taking their definition of a right as an interest that "qualifies as a right when an effective legal system treats it as such by using collective resources to defend it,"[11] and treating "rights" and

10. Ibid., e.g., pp. 39, 46, 83, 93.
11. Ibid., p. 17.

"liberty" as interchangeable terms, we are justified in deducing the following:

- If I have an interest in not taking habit-forming drugs, and
- If the state uses collective resources to stop me from taking drugs, then
- I have a right that the state use collective resources to stop me from taking drugs.

Let us stipulate that the state places me in prison in order to keep me from taking drugs (and let's set aside the fact that real states have failed to keep drugs out of prison). Since to have my rights enforced is to enjoy the protection of my liberty, by putting me in prison the state is making me free. Indeed, if the state were somehow to fail to imprison me, they would be violating my rights. (But then, if the right were not actually enforced by the state, it would be no right. Trying to follow the implications of their theory is like thinking out the implications of the elevation of evil to good by the members of "The Addams Family." Ultimately, the attempt collapses into incoherence.)

Finally, the theory Holmes and Sunstein advance collapses into circularity by page 203 of the book, which contains the first consideration of "moral ideas" since the introduction, where moral rights were dismissed in order to achieve "an enhanced clarity of focus." After maintaining for over 200 pages that rights are dependent upon power, which they defined as the power to impose punishment (again, "duties are taken seriously only when dereliction is punished by the public power drawing on the public purse"), they make the following startling admission: "The dependency of rights on power does not spell cynicism because power itself has various sources. It arises not from money or office or social status alone. It also comes from moral ideas capable of rallying organized social support."[12]

12. Ibid., p. 203.

The example they give is the civil rights movement, which brought the state into protecting the civil rights of African Americans. But if moral ideas count as a form of "power," then what is the justification for the dismissal of moral rights at the outset? Could we not say that a police officer should abstain from torturing me firstly because it is a wicked and immoral thing to do—because it is a violation of my right not to be tortured—and not *merely* because the officer fears being punished by his superiors, who, in turn, must fear being punished by their superiors? Their theory becomes circular when they incorporate "moral ideas" into their definition of power, which was offered as an alternative to moral ideas in the first place.

The point of the foregoing is not merely to pummel two harmless law professors, no matter how much they may deserve it,[13] but also to illustrate the conceptual problems inherent in recent attempts to formulate theories of rights. The problem with much contemporary rights theorizing goes deeper than the logical chaos generated by Holmes and Sunstein in their attempt to jettison traditional rights thinking. It afflicts the background understandings of rights with which Holmes and Sunstein combine their claim that all rights are "powers granted by the political community." To understand those deeper problems, I turn to the work of two other distinguished contemporary theorist of rights, Joseph Raz and Ronald Dworkin.

---

13. It should not go unremarked that *The Cost of Rights* is extraordinarily polemical, unscholarly, and nasty in its criticisms of those with differing views. For example, immediately after gallantly conceding that "Many critics of the regulatory-welfare state are in perfectly good faith" (216), they turn around to tar all critics of the welfare state with the charge of racism: "But their claim that 'positive rights' are somehow un-American and should be replaced by a policy of nonintervention is so implausible on its face that we may well wonder why it persists. What explains the survival of such a grievously inadequate way of thinking? There are many possible answers, but inherited biases—including racial prejudice, conscious and unconscious—probably play a role. Indeed, the claim that the only real liberties are the rights of property and contract can sometimes verge on a form of white separatism: prison-building should supplant Head Start. Withdrawal into gated communities should replace a politics of inclusion." (216) Their slithery charge is not only unsubstantiated, it is beneath contempt.

In his book *The Morality of Freedom*, Raz defines a right as follows: "'X has a right' if and only if X can have rights, and, other things being equal, an aspect of X's well-being (his interest) is a sufficient reason for holding some other person(s) to be under a duty."[14] Raz rejects one of the mainstays of traditional rights theory, the thesis that rights and duties are (at least normally) correlative: "A right of one person is not a duty on another. It is the ground of a duty, ground which, if not counteracted by conflicting considerations, justifies holding that other person to have a duty."[15]

Thus, for Raz, to assert a right is not necessarily to assert any duty on the part of another person, whether that duty has a negative or a positive character. Rather, asserting a right merely offers a *reason* to hold another person under a duty, but that reason may be overridden by some greater reason, and it is the balance of reasons that determines whether that person is held under a duty or not.

Similarly, the rights theorist Ronald Dworkin has defined rights as "trumps," but these "trumps" seem simply to serve as weights rather than as trumps as understood by players of card games:

> Individual rights are political trumps held by individuals. Individuals have rights when, for some reason, a collective goal is not a sufficient justification for denying them what they wish, as individuals, to have or to do, or not a sufficient justification for imposing some loss or injury upon them.[16]

Further,

No one has a political right (on my account) unless the reasons for

---

14. Joseph Raz, *The Morality of Freedom* (Oxford: Oxford University Press, 1986), p. 166.

15. Ibid., p. 171.

16. Ronald Dworkin, *Taking Rights Seriously* (Cambridge: Harvard University Press, 1978), p. xi.

giving him what he asks are stronger than some collective justification that normally provides a full political justification for a decision.[17]

When rights are grounded in this or a similar manner, they have, as Raz notes, "a dynamical character," that is to say, they change in often quite unpredictable ways; in particular, they change in ways unpredictable to the citizenry generally.[18] Thus, some citizens may have thought that they had the right "peaceably to assemble, and to petition the government for a redress of grievances" (First Amendment) or the right to "be secure in their persons, houses, papers, and effects, against unreasonable searches and seizures" (Fourth Amendment), but, without their knowledge, something had changed such that those rights articulated in the First and Fourth Amendments no longer generated any duties on the government or on their fellow citizens to allow (or refrain from prohibiting) them to assemble peace-

17. Ronald Dworkin, *Taking Rights Seriously*, p. 365. As Anthony de Jasay remarks of this theory, "In brief, it all depends on *which* reason weighs more. But what is the good of enunciating that the heavier weight outweighs the lighter one and it all depends on which is which? Manifestly, 'rights are trumps' when the balance of benefit does not outweigh them; they are not trumps when it does. But this is saying nothing more than that a card may be stronger than some other card yet weaker than a third one. It is *not* saying that the card is a trump." Anthony de Jasay, *Choice, Contract, Consent: A Restatement of Liberalism* (London: Institute of Economic Affairs, 1991), pp. 39–40. Contrast Dworkinian "rights," a mere juridical residue or afterthought capable of justifying claims only when "a collective good is not a sufficient justification for denying them what they wish," with Joel Feinberg's description of rights, "whose characteristic use and that for which they are distinctively well suited, is to be claimed, demanded, affirmed, insisted upon. They are especially sturdy objects to 'stand upon,' a most useful sort of moral furniture. Having rights, of course, makes claiming possible; but it is claiming that gives rights their special moral significance. This feature of rights is connected in a way with the customary rhetoric about what it is to be a human being. Having rights enables us to 'stand up like men,' to look others in the eye, and to feel in some fundamental way the equal of anyone." Joel Feinberg, "The Nature and Value of Rights," in *Rights, Justice, and the Bounds of Liberty: Essays in Social Philosophy* (Princeton: Princeton University Press, 1980), p. 151.

18. Joseph Raz, *The Morality of Freedom*, p. 185. As Raz explains, "They are not merely the grounds of existing duties. With changing circumstances they can generate new duties" (p. 186).

ably and petition the government for a redress of grievances or to allow them to be secure in their persons, houses, papers, and effects Let us say that some other citizens had been discovered (perhaps by the legislature) to have some new interest in overriding those rights, possibly because they were offended by the speeches given at the peaceable assemblies of their fellow citizens or because they wanted to have the persons, papers, or effects of their fellow citizens. Then, the existence of such interests might easily be construed to generate some reason(s) to hold the first group of citizens under a duty. If so, then the second group of citizens would have a right to override the rights of the first group. But even that is not a sufficient reason for the state to override the rights secured by the First and Fourth Amendments, for the balance of rights would have to be such that the rights of the second group would outweigh the first, thus generating a duty on the part of the first to submit to the second. Just as surely as interests conflict, rights will conflict, when construed in the manner of Raz, Dworkin, and their followers.

Put in more concrete terms, if I have an interest in taking your farm or in stopping you from making remarks that I consider demeaning, there is a case to be made that I have a right to take your farm or to suppress your speech, and if either the balance of reasons (Raz) or the "collective goal" (Dworkin) is weightier than your claim to your farm or to your speech, then you have a duty to submit to the confiscation of your farm or the suppression of your speech.

This might be made more clear if we consider a product of this general approach to rights, the Universal Declaration of Human Rights adopted by the United Nations in 1948. According to Article 24,

> Everyone has the right to rest and leisure, including reasonable limitation of working hours and periodic holidays with pay.

And according to Article 25,

> Everyone has the right to a standard of living adequate for the health and well-being of himself and of his family, including food, clothing, housing and medical care and necessary social services, and the right to security in the event of unemployment, sickness, disability, widowhood, old age or other lack of livelihood in circumstances beyond his control.

Let us say that Bill needs medical care and necessary social services and that Janet is a doctor. If Bill has the right to Janet's services (Article 25), but Janet has the right to rest, leisure, reasonable working hours, and periodic holidays with pay (Article 24), and those conflict (as they surely do on occasions), whose rights will be realized?[19]

One of the defenders of the "interest theory" propounded by Raz, Jeremy Waldron, rather cheerfully admits that rights construed in this manner will not only be "dynamic" but will also generate conflicts as a matter of course:

> I shall argue as follows: first, that if rights are understood along the lines of the Interest Theory propounded by Joseph Raz, then conflicts of rights must be regarded as more or less inevitable; second, that rights on this conception should be thought of, not as correlative to single duties, but as generating a multiplicity of duties; and third, that this multiplicity stands in the way of any tidy or single-minded account of the way in which the resolution of rights conflicts should be approached.[20]

Waldron takes up the challenge to such interests-as-rights (or rights-

---

19. It seems no accident that the penultimate article in this entire declaration of "human rights" is a statement of an obligation: "Everyone has duties to the community in which alone the free and full development of his personality is possible." That is to say, everyone has the right to have "duties to the community," a phrase normally interpreted to mean a duty to obey the state. Under this conception, one's rights evaporate into a duty to obey the state, which is the institution charged with determining which of many and varied conflicting interests will be fulfilled.

20. Jeremy Waldron, "Rights in Conflict," in Waldron, *Liberal Rights: Collected Papers 1981–1991* (Cambridge: Cambridge University Press, 1993), p. 203.

as-interests) theories, laid down by Maurice Cranston, a defender of a more traditional liberal rights conception. According to Cranston,

> If it is impossible for a thing to be done, it is absurd to claim it as a right. At present it is utterly impossible, and will be for a long time yet, to provide 'holidays with pay' [per Article 24, Universal Declaration of Human Rights] for everybody in the world.[21]

Cranston offered the criterion of possibility as part of a critique of those who argue that leisure, income, health care, housing, and so on are "human rights"; he does not deny that we have interests in such goods, but merely notes that "ought" implies "can" and asks how something that is impossible can be considered a right. Waldron's response to Cranston's critique of such claims trades on an equivocal use of terms rather than grappling with the very real problem that Cranston raises:

> But for each of the inhabitants of these regions, it is *not* the case that his government is unable to secure holidays with pay, or medical care, or education, or other aspects of welfare, *for him*. Indeed, it can probably do so (and does!) for a fair number of its citizens, leaving it an open question who these lucky individuals are to be. For any inhabitant of these regions, a claim might sensibly be made that his interest in basic welfare is sufficiently important to justify holding the government to be under a duty to provide it, and it would be a duty that the government is capable of performing.
>
> So, in each case, the putative right does satisfy the test of practicability. The problems posed by scarcity and underdevelopment only arise when we take all the claims of right together. It is not the duties in each individual case which demand the impossible . . . rather it is the combination of all the duties taken together which cannot be fulfilled.
>
> But one of the important features of rights discourse is that rights

---

21. Maurice Cranston, "Human Rights: Real and Supposed," in D. D. Raphael, ed., *Political Theory and the Rights of Man* (Bloomington: Indiana University Press, 1967), p. 50.

are attributed to individuals one by one, not collectively or in the aggregate.[22]

In other words, if one person could be provided with all of these goods, then every person has a right to have all of them. The error in the response is to take the idea that rights inhere in individuals and interpret it to mean that rights claims must be examined one at a time, in isolation from all other rights claims, rather than altogether. But there is nothing in the idea of individual rights that requires such an approach. The upshot of Waldron's response is that for each person whose right is respected, another must see his or her right denied, creating a "zero-sum game" of rights. But it is precisely a feature of rights that they are supposed to make social life possible, not impossible.

In John Locke's words,

> The duties of life are not at variance with one another, nor do they arm men against one another—a result which, secondly, follows of necessity from the preceding assumption, for upon it men were, as they say, by the law of nature in a state of war; so all society is abolished and all trust, which is the bond of society.[23]

Compounding the strange and unwarranted interpretation of individualism to mean claims-taken-in-isolation-and-without-regard-to-any-other-claims is the naïveté Waldron exhibits when considering as a mere detail "the open question of who these lucky individuals are to be." Does Waldron expect a lottery to be held in poor countries in which governments have the power to determine who these "lucky individuals are to be," or does he think some sort of favoritism (familial, ethnic, bribe-induced, tribal, religious, or the like) might be more likely? (The question virtually answers itself.)

Raz's and Waldron's approaches to rights effectively dispense with

---

22. Waldron, p. 207.

23. John Locke, "Essays on the Law of Nature," in *Political Essays*, ed. Mark Goldie (Cambridge: Cambridge University Press, 1997), p. 132.

rights, for a conception of rights that entails that "conflicts of rights must be regarded as more or less inevitable" still leaves us with the problem of how to decide among conflicting claims. And since each of the parties to a conflict of rights is already stipulated to have the right, then the conflict cannot be decided on the basis of rights. Some principle other than right must be invoked to resolve the conflict. In Raz's and Waldron's formulations of rights, rights become otiose, a useless ornament decorating a system of jurisprudence that seeks to order society on some other, unspecified basis.[24]

Matthew H. Kramer glosses the problems of conflict generated by such theories as follows:

> Unlike a duty to do φ and a liberty to abstain from doing φ, a duty to do φ and a duty to abstain from doing φ are not starkly contradictory. They are in conflict rather than in contradiction. Though the fulfillment of either one must rule out the fulfillment of the other, the existence of either one does not in any way preclude the existence of the other.[25]

That is to say, the two statements are not logically contradictory; only the fulfillment of the duties they enjoin is impossible. (Some) logicians may be comforted by such remarks, but the parties to social conflict probably will not be. Experience shows that political power and influence, not to mention brute force and violence, come readily to mind as likely resolutions to such conflicts, which—by stipulation—cannot be resolved on the basis of rights.

Even further along the spectrum of illiberal rights theorists is

24. "Law" and "right" are related concepts, with a complex historical connection. To reject "right" is, in effect, to reject law in favor of arbitrary will. But, as Aristotle wryly noted in *Politics*, "it is better if all these things are done in accordance with law rather than in accordance with human wish, as the latter is not a safe standard." (1272b5–8) Aristotle, *Politics*, trans. Carnes Lord (Chicago: University of Chicago Press, 1984), p. 80.

25. Matthew H. Kramer, "Rights Without Trimmings," in Matthew H. Kramer, Nigel Simmonds, and Hillel Steiner, *A Debate over Rights: Philosophical Enquiries* (New York: Oxford University Press, 2000), p. 19.

Attracta Ingram, who presents us with a "rights" theory in which rights are not merely made otiose but are also effectively annulled altogether. In *A Political Theory of Rights*, she attempts to ground "rights" on a specific theory of autonomy and criticizes traditional liberal theory on the grounds that "it neglects to specify an ideal of the person under which a scheme of constraints is derived."[26] She appeals to the autonomy-based theory of Immanuel Kant but radically collectivizes the concept of autonomy, such that the principles that result

> are not the maxims of private acts of moral law-making, but principles that command the assent of a plurality of agents. In the absence of empirical conditions favouring impartiality we must envisage the relevant assent as hypothetical. It is the assent we would give were our motives and rationality unwarped by all those traits of personal and social character that we ordinarily regard as prejudicing the pursuit of goodness or justice.[27]

What is especially noteworthy is the radical indeterminacy of the resulting principles: They are the principles that a "plurality of moral agents" who were sufficiently "unwarped" would assent to. The radical intolerance resulting from this approach is suggested in an ominous passage of the book regarding competing substantive ideals of goodness:

> There are many conceptions of happiness. Their relative merits are disputed. From the point of view of autonomy they function as so many resources from which we can choose our conception of the good, *provided only that they fall within the range of autonomy-regarding moralities*.[28] (emphasis added)

Thus, conceptions of the good that are not "autonomy-regarding" are

26. Attracta Ingram, *A Political Theory of Rights* (Oxford: Clarendon Press, 1994), p. 117.
27. Ibid., p. 153.
28. Ibid., p. 164.

not allowed. Ingram is perhaps too embarrassed by the implications of her chilling statement to address the obvious question of whether Orthodox Judaism, Roman Catholicism, Islam, or other religious (or nonreligious) belief systems provide sufficiently "autonomy-regarding" conceptions of the good for us to be allowed to choose among them. In the name of autonomy, all personal ideals are to be regulated by the collectivity. "Since the exercise of autonomy leads to incompatible personal ideals there is no option but to regulate their claims collectively in politics."[29]

Thus, we arrive at a theory of "rights" that justifies the authoritarian or totalitarian state. Alternatives to traditional liberal (and American) conceptions of rights, as we have seen, generate contradiction and incoherence; some even explicitly aim at authoritarian or even totalitarian political structures, thus not merely discombobulating rights theory but destroying it altogether.

LOGIC AND FUNCTIONALITY

The internal logic of the theories of rights offered by advocates of welfare statism such as Raz, Waldron, Holmes, and Sunstein generates contradiction, circularity, incoherence, and, as a consequence, uncertainty and irreconcilable social conflict.

What such thinkers fail to appreciate is that rights have a social function. For one thing, they have made possible the complex civilization we see around us today. Without individual rights, such complex institutions and the extended order of modern civilization would not have been possible. Social order has its requirements, and those will have their analog in the structure and the theory of rights that accompany a social order. Just as the architectural and engineering plans for a building must not contradict mathematical and physical principles if the building is to serve its function (assuming

29. Ibid., p. 166.

that its function is not to collapse on its inhabitants), so the rules of social order, including rights, must not contain contradictions or violate basic principles of inference if the social order is to serve its function—indeed, if social *order* is to exist at all.[30]

Contrary to the assertions of extreme social constructivists who believe that all institutions and practices are "social constructions," by which they mean pure assertions of will, human nature is not infinitely plastic.[31] Objective reality, including the nature of the human being, imposes on human institutions certain constraints. Histories of institutions and of concepts can be formulated and understood precisely because reality is capable of being grasped by the mind.

To say that humans are constrained in various ways or that there are coherent patterns in human history is not the same as to make claims on behalf of a grand scheme of history, in the style of G.W.F. Hegel. Even if we reject Hegel's grandiose philosophy of history (as I do), we can still acknowledge a kind of logic that shapes human

30. The analogy of social rules to architectural principles is explored at greater length by Randy Barnett in *The Structure of Liberty: Justice and the Rule of Law* (Oxford: Clarendon Press, 1998), esp. pp. 1–24. The function of laws and rules in securing social order was central to the influential approach of the seventeenth-century legal philosopher Samuel Pufendorf. As he noted, "Men are not all moved by one simple uniform desire, but by a multiplicity of desires variously combined. . . . For these reasons careful regulation and control are needed to keep them from coming into conflict with each other. . . . The conclusion is: in order to be safe, it is necessary for him to be sociable; that is to join forces with men like himself and so conduct himself towards them that they are not given even a plausible excuse for harming him, but rather become willing to preserve and promote his advantages [*commoda*]. The laws of this sociality [*socialitas*], laws which teach one how to conduct oneself to become a useful [*commodum*] member of human society, are called natural laws." Samuel Pufendorf, *On the Duty of Man and Citizen According to Natural Law*, trans. Michael Silverthorne, ed. James Tully (Cambridge: Cambridge University Press, 1991), p. 35.

31. I criticize only "extreme" social constructivists because it is undeniable that institutions are products of human action, and sometimes even of conscious human design. The error of the extremists is to believe that because social institutions are products of human action, they can be any way we choose or want them to be.

responses to problems, a logic that the philosopher Karl Popper called the "logic of the situation."[32] Without the possibility of tracing out the logic of situations, there would be little reason, if any, to listen to the explanations of political scientists, historians, military strategists, economists, or other students of human interaction; there would be no narrative to follow, no reason why, given that X was done, Y was the consequence.

If social order and cooperation are correlative to some system or systems of rights, then a conceptual formulation of such a system or systems of rights should not entail logical chaos, for that logical chaos will show up in the world of human action as social conflict and warfare rather than as social order and cooperation.

The conflicts of rights that Waldron admits is an inevitable feature of interest theories, and the infinite regress, circularity, and incoherence that are necessary features of the theory of Holmes and Sunstein, indicate that such theories do not correspond to and are not compatible with plan coordination and peaceful cooperation.

Liberal civilization requires mutual coordination and peaceful cooperation, as F. A. Hayek explains:

> What is required if the separate actions of the individuals are to result in an overall order is that they not only do not unnecessarily interfere with one another, but also that in those respects in which the success of the action of the individuals depends on some matching action by others, there will be at least a good chance that this correspondence will actually occur."[33]

Such correspondence will not occur if rights and duties are unpredictably "dynamic," nor if they generate conflicts, nor if they rest on infinite regresses or circular reasoning.

---

32. See Karl Popper, *The Poverty of Historicism* (Boston: Beacon Press, 1957), pp. 149–52.

33. F. A. Hayek, *Law, Legislation, and Liberty*, vol. I, *Rules and Order* (Chicago: University of Chicago Press, 1973), pp. 98–99.

Such an order and such coordination require a system of rights over the things of the world, as Thomas Aquinas noted in offering three reasons why property "is necessary to human life":

> First because every man is more careful to procure what is for himself alone than that which is common to many or to all: since each would shirk the labor and leave to another that which concerns the community, as happens where there is a great number of servants. Secondly, because human affairs are conducted in more orderly fashion if each man is charged with taking care of some particular thing himself, whereas there would be confusion if everyone had to look after any one thing indeterminately. Thirdly, because a more peaceful state is ensured to man if each one is contented with his own. Hence it is to be observed that quarrels arise more frequently where there is no division of the things possessed.[34]

The "more peaceful state" ensured to man is a function of the system of rights that accompanies it. A peaceful state requires a fundamental stability of property; it requires that rights not have Raz's "dynamic character" or generate Waldron's inevitable conflicts. As James Madison noted in *Federalist* Number 62, the effects of a "mutable policy" (for "mutable" read "dynamic") "poisons the blessings of liberty itself."

> It will be of little avail to the people that the laws are made by men of their own choice if the laws be so voluminous that they cannot be read, or so incoherent that they cannot be understood; if they be repealed or revised before they are promulgated, or undergo such incessant changes that no man, who knows what the law is today, can guess what it will be tomorrow. Law is defined to be a rule of action; but how can that be a rule, which is little known, and less fixed?
>
> Another effect of public instability is the unreasonable advantage it gives to the sagacious, the enterprising, and the moneyed few over

---

34. St. Thomas Aquinas, *Summa Theologica*, Iia, IIae, Q. 66, trans. Fathers of the English Dominican Province (Westminster, Md.: Christian Classics, 1981), vol. III, p. 1471. Thomas represents in this regard, as in many others, a great advance over Aristotle's account of property in *The Politics*, esp. Bk. 2, Chaps. 3, 4, 5, and 7.

the industrious and uninformed mass of the people. Every new regulation concerning commerce or revenue, or in any manner affecting
the value of the different species of property, presents a new harvest
to those who watch the change, and can trace its consequences; a
harvest, reared not by themselves, but by the toils and cares of the
great body of their fellow-citizens. This is a state of things in which it
may be said with some truth that laws are made for the *few*, not for
the *many*.[35]

What I propose is to look at the history of the development of the
traditional theories of rights that Raz, Waldron, and Holmes and
Sunstein seek to replace and to see how it reveals a convergence of
rights theory with institutions of social cooperation and coordination.
By showing how liberal rights theories correspond to and support
liberal civilization, we may see why and how they are superior to the
proposed replacements offered by philosophical advocates of dynamic and conflicting rights.[36]

OBJECTIVE RIGHT, SUBJECTIVE RIGHT, AND LAW

It is beyond the scope of this essay to offer a detailed historical
account of the development of rights, of their roots in Greek philos-

35. James Madison, "Concerning the Constitution of the Senate with Regard to
the Qualifications of the Members, the Manner of Appointing Them, the Equality
of Representation, the Number of the Senators, and the Duration of their Appoint-
ments," No. 62, in James Madison, Alexander Hamilton, and John Jay, *The Federalist
Papers* (New York: Penguin Books, 1987), p. 368.

36. It should be remembered that recognizing that some system of rights is
integral to a social order is not the same as claiming that those rights are always
respected and never violated. That even broadly liberal societies still suffer from
criminal aggression—both from states and from freelance criminals—is not necessarily an indictment of the liberal system of rights that seeks to outlaw such violations
of rights. Some rights schemes may be unstable and self-destructive when attempts
are made to put them into practice (the catastrophe of classical socialism is a good
example of an unstable social order), but in general, liberal rights have shown
themselves to be stable, even in the face of violations by state officials and other
criminals.

ophy, Roman law, and medieval theology and philosophy, so I will offer instead a sketchy presentation of the outlines of that history, for the purpose of demonstrating the coherence of the concepts of justice and rights that emerged.

Objective right, or the right ordering of society, is intimately related to subjective right, or the rights of the individuals who make up a social order. Objective right is what we could call the right arrangement of things. It refers to how things ought to be: thus, it is right that X and Y should obtain. Subjective right refers to the rights of the acting subjects who constitute a social order: thus, it is A's right that B happen (or not happen).[37] As Brian Tierney notes in connection with the connection of objective right with subjective rights,

> to affirm a right ordering of human relationships is to imply a structure of rights and duties. In propounding a system of jurisprudence one can emphasize either the objective pattern of relationships or the implied rights and duties of persons to one another—and then again one can focus on either the rights or the duties.[38]

Objective right and subjective right are not only logically compatible, but in a well-ordered theory of justice they should also be complementary.

Whereas the approaches of Raz, Waldron, and Holmes and Sunstein would set the right ordering society (objective right) and the rights of individuals (subjective right) at odds, the classical tradition of rights thinking was premised on their unity, complementarity, or mutual implication.

One of the most significant occurrences in the history of rights theory was the fusion of Aristotelian ethical philosophy with the legal

---

37. These categories are related, but not reducible, to Aristotle's categories of universal and particular justice. See the discussion in Fred Miller Jr., *Nature, Justice, and Rights in Aristotle's Politics* (Oxford: Clarendon Press, 1995), esp. pp. 68–74.

38. Brian Tierney, *The Idea of Natural Rights* (Atlanta: Scholars Press, 1997), p. 33.

categories of the Roman law, as James Gordley has brilliantly shown in his book *The Philosophical Origins of Modern Contract Doctrine*.[39]

For Aristotle, justice is understood as "that disposition which renders men apt to do just things, and which causes them to act justly and to wish what is just."[40] Justice or right is oriented to the object of action, that is, to the thing done. In contrast, the Roman law tradition emphasized not so much the thing done as the recipient's claim, as one might expect of the law of a great commercial civilization. The Roman law was transmitted to the civilizations that succeeded Rome through the *Digest of Justinian*, a codification of centuries of Roman law that was drawn up in the sixth century C.E. under the direction of the jurist Tribonian and rediscovered in the Latin west in the eleventh century.

The definition of justice offered by the Roman jurist Ulpian was prominently offered as authoritative in the *Digest*:

> Justice is a steady and enduring will to render unto everyone his right. 1. The basic principles of right are: to live honorably, not to harm another person, to render to each his own. 2. Practical wisdom in matters of right is an awareness of God's and men's affairs, knowledge of justice and injustice.[41]

In the thirteenth century C.E., Thomas Aquinas, the great synthesizer, undertook to synthesize these approaches in his *Summa Theologica*; Ulpian's definition, he stated, is compatible with Aristotle's

---

39. James Gordley, *The Philosophical Origins of Modern Contract Doctrine* (Oxford: Clarendon Press, 1991). Gordley focuses most of his attention on the late scholastics of the Spanish natural law school, but the movement is already perceptible in the work of Thomas Aquinas, as Annabel S. Brett notes in *Liberty, Right, and Nature: Individual Rights in Later Scholastic Thought* (Cambridge: Cambridge University Press, 1997), pp. 89–97.

40. Aristotle, *Nicomachean Ethics*, V, i., 1129a8–9, trans. H. Rackham (Cambridge: Harvard University Press, 1934), p. 253.

41. *The Digest of Justinian*, trans. and ed. Alan Watson (Philadelphia: University of Pennsylvania Press, 1998), I, i, 10.

if understood aright. For since every virtue is a habit that is the principle of a good act, a virtue must needs be defined by means of the good act bearing on the matter proper to that virtue. Now the proper matter of justice consists of those things that belong to our intercourse with other men. . . . Hence the act of justice in relation to its proper matter and object is indicated in the words, *Rendering to each one his right*, since, as Isidore says (Etym. x), *a man is said to be just because he respects the rights* (jus) *of others.*[42]

Thus, right is something due to another person, something that belongs to that person and to which he or she can make a just claim.

As Annabel Brett notes, however, although Thomas attempts to reconcile the definitions of justice offered by Aristotle and by Ulpian, "the primary and theoretically important sense of iustum in Aquinas . . . remains that of 'just action.'"[43] A theoretical formulation of subjective right remained for the Spanish Scholastics to formulate and transmit to later generations of legal theorists and practitioners.

Here it is important to stress the significance of the work of philosophers in rationalizing legal practices, for the abstract formulation of these principles helped to create the abstract order that characterizes modern society. Such abstract formulation is inherently well suited or oriented toward a normative order of universality and equality, for abstract formulations do not take account of the concrete characteristics (race, birth, color, wealth, and so on) of the persons who fit particular legal categories (buyer, seller, parent, child, and so on).

For this reason, philosophy is particularly well suited to the formulation of the principles of liberalism. The absurdities to which collectivist/communitarian philosophy has been led in recent decades shows that it is at least remarkably difficult to formulate abstractly principles that divide human beings into separated "incom-

42. Thomas Aquinas, IIa, IIae, Q. 58, p. 1429.
43. Annabel S. Brett, *Liberty, Right, and Nature*, p. 92.

mensurable" communities, classes, nations, or races, as communitarian critics of liberalism seek to do.[44]

44. One noted critic of traditional liberal principles, Michael Sandel, has argued
in his *Liberalism and the Limits of Justice* (Cambridge: Cambridge University Press,
1982) that selves need not be "individuated in advance," but should "comprehend a
wider subject than the individual alone, whether a family or tribe or city or class or
nation or people," and "to this extent they define a community in a constitutive
sense." (172) In other words, rather than speaking merely of Mary and William and
Tadd and Sylvia, we would speak of the "self" composed of Mary, William, Tadd,
and Sylvia. What Sandel is arguing is that an epistemological principle can be
transformed into an ontological principle: "this notion of community [the constitutive
conception] describes a framework of self-understandings that is distinguishable
from and in some sense prior to the sentiments and dispositions of individuals within
the framework." (174) Because shared understandings are necessary for our self-
understanding, i.e., because they are asserted to be an epistemic criterion for self-
knowledge, it is asserted that these shared understandings are constitutive of our
identity and that therefore "the bounds of the self are no longer fixed, individuated
in advance and given prior to experience." (183) This move is unjustified. As John
Haldane remarks, "even if this were granted it would not follow from it that subjects
of these relationships are anything other than distinct persons. To suppose otherwise
is to infer fallaciously that epistemological considerations enter into the constitution
of the object known." ("Individuals and the Theory of Justice," *Ratio* XXVII 2 [De-
cember 1985]: pp. 189–96.) This is an old debate, and the outlines can be traced
quite clearly in the debate between the "Latin Averroists," notably Siger of Brabant,
and St. Thomas Aquinas over whether there is one "intellective soul" for all of
mankind. The Averroists argued that for two individuals to know the same thing,
they have to have the same form impressed by the agent intellect into the same
material (or possible) intellect; to know the same form, they must share the same
material intellect. See Siger of Brabant, "On the Intellective Soul," in *Medieval
Philosophy: From St. Augustine to Nicholas of Cusa*, ed. John F. Wippel and Allan
B. Wolter, O.F.M. (London: Collier Macmillan Publishers, 1969), pp. 358–65. As
some sources note, it was reported in the thirteenth century that this thesis had
radical implications for the moral responsibilities of the individual: If Peter was
saved, then I will be saved too, as we share the same intellective soul. So I am free
to engage in whatever sinful behavior I wish, in the knowledge that I will be saved
nonetheless. Thomas responded that the impressed intelligible species is not literally
the very form of the thing raised to a higher level of intelligibility but rather that *by
which* we know the thing: "It is . . . one thing which is understood both by me and
by you. But it is understood by me in one way and by you in another, that is, by
another intelligible species. And my understanding is one thing, and yours, another;
and my intellect is one thing, and yours another." Thomas Aquinas, *On the Unity of
the Intellect Against the Averroists* (Milwaukee: Marquette University Press, 1968),
chap. V, par. 112, p. 70. The issue is canvassed in Herbert Davidson, *Alfarabi,
Avicenna, and Averroes on Intellect* (Oxford: Oxford University Press, 1994).

By attempting to substitute for individual responsibility a concept of collective responsibility, collectivists and coercive communitarians undermine the very thing they often seek to support, which is deliberative and democratic decision-making, for by erasing the distinction among persons, they eliminate at the same time the very point of deliberation, which is for numerically individuated persons to decide on a common course. Thomas pointed out the problem in concluding from the observed fact of common ideas and attachments that those who share the same ideas and attachments make up one self:

> If . . . the intellect does not belong to this man in such a way that it is truly one with him, but is united to him only through phantasms or as a mover, the will will not be in this man, but in the separate intellect. And so this man will not be the master of his act, nor will any act of his be praiseworthy or blameworthy. That is to destroy the principles of moral philosophy. Since this is absurd and contrary to human life (for it would not be necessary to take counsel or to make laws), it follows that the intellect is united to us in such a way that it and we constitute what is truly one being.[45]

Democratic deliberation requires individualism and the abstract formulation of claims of justice; to deny the latter is to deny the former.

DOMINIUM, RESPONSIBILITY, AND PROPERTY

The concepts of individualism and of responsibility have a history, and an examination of that history is likely to lead to greater understanding of the concepts themselves. The debates over property that divided the papal and imperial parties provided great opportunities for the philosophers who enlisted on one side or the other to clarify the concept of rights. The key issue was what was meant by *dominium* ("mastery" or "ownership"), a term that was to prove of great significance to the development of rights talk.

The issue of dominium figured prominently in the debates con-

---

45. Thomas Aquinas, *On the Unity of the Intellect Against the Averroists*, chap. II, par. 82, p. 57.

cerning the relations between the church as a corporate body and the empire, notably in the debate over "apostolic poverty"—over whether priests, and therefore the church, were required to abjure claims to property. The advocates of the imperial power were eager to argue that the church should not own lands and other wealth, and naturally the German emperors were quite happy to relieve the church of their burdens. John XXII had responded in 1322 C.E. in the bull *Ad conditorem canonum* against the arguments for apostolic poverty by pointing out the inseparability of the right of use in consumable goods (which priests, as human beings, surely enjoyed) from the right of ownership; to exercise the right to consume is necessarily to exclude, and therefore to exercise a claim of a right to exclude.[46] Marsilius of Padua responded in 1324 C.E. and in the process clarified the meaning of property or ownership (dominium): "In its strict sense, this term means the principal power to lay claim to something rightfully acquired . . . ; that is, the power of a person who . . . wants to allow no one else to handle that thing without his, the owner's, express consent, while he owns it."[47] Most notably, Marsilius grounded the entire edifice of jurisdiction over resources in the world on one's domimium over oneself:

> Again, this term "ownership" [dominium] is used to refer to the human will or freedom in itself with its organic executive or motive power unimpeded. For it is through these that we are capable of certain acts

46. See the discussion in Brian Tierney, "Marsilius on Rights," *Journal of the History of Ideas* LII, no. 1 (Jan.–March, 1991): pp. 3–17, and Brian Tierney, *The Idea of Natural Rights*, pp. 93–130. Compare the modern economist of property rights Yoram Barzel: "The ability to consume commodities, including those necessary to sustain life, implies the possession of rights over them." *Economic Analysis of Property Rights* (Cambridge: Cambridge University Press, 1989), p. 62.

47. Marsilius of Padua, *The Defender of the Peace: The Defensor Pacis*, trans. Alan Gewirth (New York: Harper and Row, 1956), discourse II, chap. XII, 13, p. 192. I have omitted from the quotation material relating to Marsilius's claim that priests have voluntarily taken vows of poverty, which was a central part of the claim of the imperial party on this matter.

and their opposites. It is for this reason too that man alone among the animals is said to have ownership or control of his acts; this control belongs to him by nature, it is not acquired through an act of will or choice.[48]

The issue received perhaps its most clear and powerful formulation in the famous debates over the treatment of the Indians by the Spanish empire. The proto-liberal thinkers of the School of Salamanca, from whom so much liberal thinking was to emerge (including the morality of private property, the justice of the market price and of the charging of interest, the role of contracts in regulating production and exchange, and the contractual nature of political society),[49] initiated a debate over the proper status and treatment of the Indians, in the process articulating a theory of universal individual rights.[50] Much of the dispute drew on the earlier debates concerning the Crusades and whether it was just to dispossess "infidels" from their lands, wealth, and political systems. A seminal text in this context was a statement of Pope Innocent IV (issued c. 1250 c.e.) on the

48. Marsilius of Padua, discourse II, chap. XII, 16, p. 193.

49. See, for example, Joseph Schumpeter, *History of Economic Analysis* (Oxford: Oxford University Press, 1954), who highlights the significance of Luis de Molina's views on the importance of free prices, since "we are not as a rule in the habit of looking to the scholastics for the origin of the theories that are associated with nineteenth-century laissez-faire liberalism" (p. 99); Alejandro Chafuen, *Christians for Freedom: Late-Scholastic Economics* (San Francisco: Ignatius Press, 1986); and Quentin Skinner, *The Foundations of Modern Political Thought*, vol. II, *The Age of Reformation* (Cambridge: Cambridge University Press, 1978), pp. 135–73.

50. As Blandine Kriegel notes, "In his *De Indis* of 1539, Vitoria maintained that Indians had the same right to liberty and property as all other human beings and that a number of rights can be deduced logically from human nature itself." Blandine Kriegel, "Rights and Natural Law," in *New French Thought: Political Philosophy*, ed. Mark Lilla (Princeton: Princeton University Press, 1994), p. 155. Brian Tierney has suggested that Francisco de Vitoria may have been directly influenced by Marsilius, for "*the Defensor Pacis* was certainly well known at Paris in the years Vitoria studied there. One difficulty is that Catholic authors usually referred to Marsilius by name only when they intended to disagree with him. When they wanted to borrow his ideas they preferred not to mention such a questionable source." Tierney, "Marsilius on Rights," p. 5.

rights of non-Christians, in which the Pope drew inspiration from the Sermon on the Mount.

> I maintain . . . that lordship, possession and jurisdiction can belong to infidels licitly and without sin, for these things were made not only for the faithful but for every rational creature as has been said. For he makes his sun to rise on the just and the wicked and he feeds the birds of the air, Matthew c.5, c.6. Accordingly we say that it is not licit for the pope or the faithful to take away from infidels their belongings or their lordships or jurisdictions because they possess them without sin.[51]

Francisco de Vitoria, in his famous essay *De Indis*, argued that the Indian "barbarians" were "true masters" and therefore "may not be dispossessed without due cause."[52] For "if the barbarians were not true masters before the arrival of the Spaniards, it can only have been on four possible grounds," which he lists as "that they were either sinners (*peccatores*), unbelievers (*infideles*), madmen (*amentes*), or insensate (*insensati*)."[53] The first two grounds are dismissed as not sufficient to deny rights, for it was recognized that even sinners and unbelievers can have rights; the third, although a sufficient ground for denying rights (dominion), is inapplicable to the Indians, for "they

51. Innocent IV, "On *Decretales*, 3.34.8, *Quod Super, Commentaria* (c. 1250), fol. 429–30," in *The Crisis of Church and State, 1050–1300*, ed. Brian Tierney (Toronto: University of Toronto Press, 1988), p. 153. The primary passage cited by Innocent bears greater mention: "You have heard that it was said, 'You shall love your neighbor and hate your enemy.' But I say to you, Love your enemies and pray for those who persecute you, so that you may be sons of your Father who is in heaven; for he makes his sun rise on the evil and the good, and sends rain on the just and on the unjust. For if you love those who love you, what reward have you? Do not even the tax collectors do the same?" (Matthew 5:43, Revised Standard Version).

52. Francisco de Vitoria, "On the American Indians," in *Political Writings*, ed. Anthony Pagden and Jeremy Lawrence (Cambridge: Cambridge University Press, 1991), p. 240.

53. Ibid., p. 240.

are not in point of fact madmen, but have judgment like other men."[54] (Whether the fourth is sufficient to deny "civil rights of ownership" Vitoria leaves to "the experts on Roman law," but he denies that the Indians are mad or irrational, as shown by their cities, their laws, marriages, religion, and so on.[55])

What are most noteworthy in this context are the criteria that Vitoria sets out for being "true masters," that is, masters—or owners—of themselves and their properties.

> *Irrational creatures cannot have any dominion*, for dominion is a legal right (*dominium est ius*), as Conrad Summenhart himself admits. Irrational creatures cannot have legal rights; therefore they cannot have any dominion. The minor premise is proved by the fact that irrational creatures cannot be victims of an injustice (*inuria*), and therefore cannot have legal rights: this assumption is proved in turn by considering the fact that to deprive a wolf or a lion of its prey is no injustice against the beast in question, any more than to shut out the sun's light by drawing the blinds is an injustice against the sun. And this is confirmed by the absurdity of the following argument: that if brutes had dominion, then any person who fenced off grass from deer would be committing a theft, since he would be stealing food without its owner's permission.
>
> And again, wild animals have no rights over their own bodies (*dominium sui*); still less, then, can they have rights over other things. . . . only rational creatures have mastery over their own actions (*dominium sui actus*), as Aquinas shows . . . [a person is master of his own actions insofar as he is able to make choices between one course and another; hence, as Aquinas says in the same passage, we are not masters as regards our appetite or our own destiny, for example]. If,

54. Ibid., p. 250.
55. Ibid., pp. 249–50. Vitoria also notes that, even were it to be conceded, *arguendo*, that the Indians suffered from "mental incapacity," any power the Spaniards might exercise over them would apply only "if everything is done for the benefit and good of the barbarians, and not merely for the profit of the Spaniards" (p. 291).

then, brutes have no dominion over their own actions, they can have no dominion over other things.[56]

To have mastery over one's own actions, that is, *dominium*,[57] is to "be able to make a choice between one course and another," and this ability to choose is, in effect, what allows us to "own" our actions, that is, to have them truly attributed to us.[58] To be a "true master" is

56. Ibid., pp. 247–48. (The passage in brackets does not appear in some editions of Vitoria's works.)

57. For the complex relationship between power, right, law, and property, as expressed in the terms *dominium, lex,* and *ius,* see Richard Tuck, *Natural Rights Theories: Their Origins and Development* (Cambridge: Cambridge University Press, 1979), but see also the criticism in Brian Tierney, "Tuck on Rights: Some Medieval Problems," *History of Political Thought* IV, no. 3 (Winter 1983): pp. 429–39. Tierney claims that the use of *dominium* is more complex in the medieval context than Tuck believes, although this is less significant in the context of the later thinkers dealt with here; Tierney also suggests an alternative route to that sketched by Tuck for a medieval development of "a possessive theory of rights," starting with "Innocent IV's defence of the rights of infidels to property and jurisdiction, and the assertion attributed to Alexander of Hales that natural law actually dictated the institution of private property among fallen men" (p. 440). Tierney suggests a direct route to a "possessive theory of rights," starting from the declaration of Innocent IV and leading to "the Indies debates of Las Casas and Sepúlveda."

58. It is noteworthy that the idea of personal responsibility intrudes even in cases in which the self-proprietorship of the actor is denied. Consider the Roman law of noxal actions: "Noxal actions lie when slaves commit delicts—theft, robbery, loss, or contempt. The actions give the condemned owner an option to pay the damages as assessed in money or to make noxal surrender of the slave." *Justinian's Institutes,* trans. and introduction by Peter Birks and Grant McLeod (London: Duckworth, 1987), 4.8, p. 137. Ulpian noted the central role of moral responsibility for misdeeds on the part of either the master or the slave: "If a slave has killed with his owner's knowledge, the owner is liable in full; for he himself is deemed to have done the killing, but if he did not know, the action is noxal; for he should not be held liable for his slave's misdeed beyond handing him over noxally." *The Digest of Justinian,* op. cit., IX, 4, 2. The Roman law scholar Barry Nichols argues that "The liability was that of the wrongdoer, and the injured person could take vengeance on him. . . . The true character of this noxal liability is plain from the rule that it followed the wrongdoer (*noxa caput sequitur*). This meant that if the slave was, for example, manumitted before the action was brought, he himself was liable to an ordinary action; or if he were sold, the noxal action lay against his new owner." Nichols, *An Introduction to Roman Law* (Oxford: Clarendon Press, 1991), p. 223.

to be an agent who can "own" his or her actions, that is, one to whom the actions can be attributed and who therefore can be said to be responsible for those actions and therefore entitled as a matter of justice or right to take those actions necessary to fulfill his or her moral obligations, both to others and to self (minimally, that entails self-preservation). According to Vitoria: "Every Indian is a man and thus is capable of attaining salvation or damnation"; "Every man is a person and is the master of his body and possessions"; "Inasmuch as he is a person, every Indian has free will, and, consequently, is the master of his actions"; "By natural law, every man has the right to his own life and to physical and mental integrity."[59]

The core of the arguments of Innocent IV, Vitoria, John Locke, and other pioneers of the theory of rights of self-propriety, as of their followers up to the present time, is a recognition that other humans are not simply mobile machines, automata, or insensate brutes, but acting agents to whom choice and responsibility may be attributed. The debate between Bartolomé de Las Casas and Juan Ginés de Sepúlveda in 1550 on the status of the Indians revolved largely around the intellectual and moral capacities of the Indians. As Las Casas argued,

> Now if we shall have shown that among our Indians of the western and southern shores (granting that we call them barbarians and that they are barbarians) there are important kingdoms, large numbers of people who live settled lives in a society, great cities, kings, judges and laws, persons who engage in commerce, buying, selling, lending, and the other contracts of the law of nations, will it not stand proved that the Reverend Doctor Sepúlveda has spoken wrongly and viciously against peoples like these, either out of malice or ignorance of Aris-

59. These statements are drawn from a variety of Vitoria's writings and are collected in Luciano Pereña Vicente, ed., *The Rights and Obligations of Indians and Spaniards in the New World, According to Francisco de Vitoria* (Salamanca: Universidad Pontifica de Salamanca, 1992); they are to be found on p. 17 of Vicente's works.

totle's teaching, and, therefore, has falsely and perhaps irreparably slandered them before the entire world?[60]

The issue was of more than academic interest, for had it been proven that the Indians were the "natural slaves" described by Aristotle in the *Politics*,[61] then the Spaniards would have been justified in applying to them the direction that they were incapable of providing themselves. By arguing that the Indians were indeed fully human and were capable of, and indeed were actively exercising, self-direction, Las Casas, following Vitoria before him, sought to refute the claims of the Spanish slaveholders and affirm the rights of the Indians to their lives, liberties, and properties. The *proper* relationship between the Spaniards and the Indians, Vitoria and Las Casas insisted, was persuasion in religion and consent-based free trade in material affairs.[62]

60. Bartolomé de Las Casas, *In Defense of the Indians*, trans. Stafford Poole (Dekalb, Ill.: Northern Illinois University Press, 1992), p. 42. Las Casas concluded his work with a moving plea: "The Indians are our brothers, and Christ has given his life for them. Why, then, do we persecute them with such inhuman savagery when they do not deserve such treatment? The past, because it cannot be undone, must be attributed to our weakness, provided that what has been taken unjustly is restored" (p. 362).

61. See the discussion in Aristotle, *Politics*, bk. I, chaps. 4–7, pp. 39–44.

62. In his *De Unico Vocationis Modo*, Las Casas praised mutual advantage over exploitation: "Worldly, ambitious men who sought wealth and pleasure placed their hope in obtaining gold and silver by the labor and sweat, even through very harsh slavery, oppression, and death, of not only innumerable people but of the greater part of humanity. . . . And the insolence and madness of these men became so great that they did not hesitate to allege that the Indians were beasts or almost beasts, and publicly defamed them. Then they claimed that it was just to subject them to our rule by war, or to hunt them like beasts and then reduce them to slavery. Thus they could make use of the Indians at their pleasure. But the truth is that very many of the Indians were able to govern themselves in monastic, economic, and political life. They could teach us and civilize us, however, and even more, would dominate us by natural reason as the Philosopher said speaking of Greeks and barbarians." Cited in Lewis Hanke, *All Mankind Is One: A Study of the Disputation between Bartolomé de las Casas and Juan Ginés Sepúlveda on the Religious and Intellectual Capacity of the American Indians* (Dekalb, Ill.: Northern Illinois University Press, 1974), p. 157.

The common humanity of Indians and Spaniards, and therefore of any and all who might meet on a basis of unequal technological, military, or other power, provided a ground for recognition of a common set of rights. But why should a common nature entail common rights? Lobsters share a common nature, but there is no justice among lobsters, still less rights. Even if a lobster can "recognize" another creature *as* a lobster, there is no mutual recognition of moral agents, no sense that "this is an agent capable of choice, as am I," nor that "this is an agent deserving of some kind of respect." The recognition of humans as choosers, as agents who can "own" their actions and be responsible for them, and who have purposes and goals of their own, which may or may not coincide with yours, involves a special kind of recognition and comportment altogether different from that appropriate to inanimate or nonrational entities.

IDENTITY, KNOWLEDGE, RIGHTS, AND JUSTICE

The idea of dominium, of personal responsibility, of an ability to "own" our acts, is central to the development of the idea of rights, and to the extension of the concept of rights to ever-wider categories of human beings.

That idea of responsibility is ultimately founded on the idea of the dominium one has over one's body. Bodies are scarce; there is only one per person. If one person were to get more than one body, that would necessarily leave at least one person without a body. That is why referring to one's *own* body is redundant; "one's own body" denotes nothing more than "one's body" and differs from the former in connotation only by emphasis.[63]

63. In the course of this chapter, I articulate and defend a theory of personal identity that, although perhaps not superior in every respect to every other theory, provides a superior foundation for a *political* theory of justice. Various other thinkers have articulated theories of personal identity that are not dependent upon the identity or continuity of bodies. Notable among them is Derek Parfit, who, in his *Reasons*

The scarcity of bodies entails that if they are to be used or, es-
chewing instrumentalist language, if their spatio-temporal dispositions are to be determined, choices must be made. The law of contradiction, "the most certain of all principles,"[64] creates a problem of
decision: "It is impossible for the same attribute at once to belong
and not to belong to the same thing and in the same relation."[65] A
body cannot be reading in the Bodleian Library at the same time that
it is drinking in the King's Arms or picking corn on an Iowa farm.
Scarcity arises from the transposition of the law of contradiction into
the context of choice. Rights arise from the transposition of scarcity
into the context of justice. Rights are the moral and legal instruments
by which scarcity problems are addressed, that is, by which agents
are informed as to who is entitled to the use of a scarce resource
under what conditions.

The centrality of dominium to personal identity, and thus to iden-
tifying who has jurisdiction over what body, was clearly stated during
the English Civil War by the Levellers, a group that exerted a great
influence on later English and American political thought. One of
their more eloquent leaders, Richard Overton, appealed to rights to
defend religious liberty in a pamphlet of 1646:

> To every individual in nature is given an individual property by nature
> not to be invaded or usurped by any. For every one, as he is himself,
> so he has a self-propriety, *else could he not be himself*; and on this no
> second may presume to deprive any of without manifest violation and
> affront to the very principles of nature and of the rules of equity and

---

and Persons (1986), argues that "personal identity is not what matters" and that "what
matters" is "psychological connectedness and/or continuity with the right kind of
cause . . . [that] could be any kind of cause" (p. 215). My reasons for preferring a
corporeal criterion of personal identity, and why such corporeal identity matters, are
set forth in the course of this chapter.

64. Aristotle, *The Metaphysics*, trans. Hugh Tredennick (Cambridge: Harvard
University Press, 1933), IV, iii, 9, 1005b19, p. 161.

65. Ibid., IV, iii, 9, 1005b20–23. The law of contradiction and the law of the
excluded middle are, in the current context, equivalent.

justice between man and man. Mine and thine cannot be, except this be. No man has power over my rights and liberties, and I over no man's. I may be but an individual, enjoy my self and my self-propriety and may right my self no more than my self, or presume any further; if I do, I am an encroacher and an invader upon another man's right— to which I have no right. For by natural birth all men are equally and alike born to like propriety, liberty and freedom; and as we are delivered of God by the hand of nature into this world, every one with a natural, innate freedom and propriety—as it were writ in the table of every man's heart, never to be obliterated—even so are we to live, everyone equally and alike to enjoy his birthright and privilege; even all whereof God by nature has made him free.[66] (emphasis added)

Such "self-propriety" was based on the recognition of the choice and freedom that individuals exercise over their own bodies. Notably, it served as the philosophical justification for the still current resister's strategy of "going limp" when arrested by state agents, as Overton argued in refusing to walk to prison when ordered to do so:

My *Leggs* were borne as free as the rest of my *Body*, and therefore I

---

66. Richard Overton, "An Arrow Against All Tyrants and Tyranny," in *The English Levellers*, ed. Andrew Sharp (Cambridge: Cambridge University Press, 1998), p. 55. Sharp has modernized spelling, punctuation, and grammar. Interestingly, the phrase "right my self no more than my self" is "write my self no more than my self" in the excerpted version of the essay in G. E. Aylmer, ed., *The Levellers in the English Revolution* (Ithaca, N.Y.: Cornell University Press, 1975), p. 68, which has a more poetic ring to it and may be more true to Overton's style. It is worth noting that Overton is not endorsing unrestricted "egotism," or the right of each to whatever he or she can get. Rather, it is a right to equality: "No man has power over my rights and liberties, and I over no man's." On the relationship between self-proprietorship and freedom of conscience, see the discussion of Overton and other Levellers, as well as of John Locke and James Madison, in George H. Smith, "Philosophies of Toleration," in *Atheism, Ayn Rand, and Other Heresies* (Buffalo: Prometheus Press, 1991), pp. 97–129. Madison expressed the basis of property in conscience when he wrote, of every individual, that "He has a property of peculiar value in his religious opinions and the free communication of them." James Madison, "Property," *National Gazette*, March 27, 1792, in *The Papers of James Madison*, ed. R. A. Rutland and others (Charlottesville: University Press of Virginia, 1983), pp. 266–68, quotation from p. 266.

scorne that *Leggs, or Armes, or hands of mine* should do them any *villeine-Service,* for as I am a *Freeman by birth,* so I am resolved to live and dye, both in heart word and deed, in substance and in shew.[67]

Overton was quite cruelly dragged to prison as a consequence. His remarks on this experience remind us of the clear relationship of self-propriety and moral agency:

> But in case you object, that I knew well enough, that if I would not go, they would carrie me, therefore it had been better for me to have gone, then to have exposed my selfe to their cruelty, I answer, 1. If I had known they would have hanged me, must I therefore have hanged my selfe? 2. A good conscience had rather run the hazard of cruelty then to abate an hairesbreadth of contestation and opposition against illegality, injustice, and tyranny. 3. If they had had any legall jurisdiction over my leggs, then at their Commands my leggs were bound to obey: And then, (in that case) I confesse it had been better to obey, then to have exposed my person to the cruelty of threatening mercilesse Gaolers: But being free from their Jurisdiction *from the Crowne of my head to the Soale of my foote,* I know no reason, why I should foote it for them, or in any the least dance any attendance to their *Arbitrary Warrants;* their Lordships may put up their pipes, except they will play to the *good old tune of the Law of the Land,* otherwise their Orders and Warrants are never like to have the service of my leggs or feet, for they were never bred to tread in their *Arbitrary Steps,* but I shall leave *their Orders* and *their execution to themselves.* And therefore, Sir, concerning that action of mine, I shall continue in the said esteeme thereof, till my defense be made voide, and it be legally proved, that by the Law of the Land, *I* was bound to set one legge before another in attendance to that Order.[68]

Regardless of the consequences, Overton retained the control over his own legs. His actions remained his own.

The rather better known philosopher of rights, John Locke, con-

---

67. Richard Overton, "The Commoner's Complaint," in *Tracts on Liberty in the Puritan Revolution, 1638–1647,* vol. III, ed. W. Haller (New York: Columbia University Press, 1943), pp. 371–95, material quoted is on p. 381.

68. Ibid., p. 382.

sidered the relation between "person" and "self" in his *Essay Concerning Human Understanding*:

> Any substance vitally united to the present thinking Being, is a part of that very *same self* which now is: Any thing united to it by a consciousness of former Actions makes also a part of the *same self*, which is the same both then and now.
>
> *Person*, as I take it, is the name for this *self*. Where-ever a Man finds, what he calls *himself*, there I think another may say is the same *Person*. It is a Forensick Term appropriating Actions and their Merit; and so only belongs to intelligent Agents capable of a Law, and Happiness and Misery. This personality extends it *self* beyond present Existence to what is past, only by consciousness, whereby it becomes concerned and accountable, owns and imputes to it self past Actions, just upon the same ground, and for the same reason, that it does the present.[69]

It is clear from his remarks in *The Second Treatise* that Locke identified the person with an animated body. After claiming that "every Man has a *Property* in his own *Person*," he immediately clarifies this by explaining that "This no Body has any Right to but himself. The *Labour* of his Body, and the *Work* of his Hands, we may say, are properly his."[70] Each person is an individual and the owner of his or her acts, which are the acts of an animated body. The body is the seat of one's personhood, one's personhood is achieved by the acts that one owns, and the responsibility for those acts is the foundation for one's rights, for the reason that hindering another from fulfilling his or her obligations is precisely to hinder that person from doing what is right, and therefore to act contrary to right.

Given that human beings are embodied persons, ascribing personal responsibility for one's acts means ascribing them to some*body*.

---

69. John Locke, *An Essay Concerning Human Understanding*, ed. Peter H. Nidditch (1684; Oxford: Clarendon Press, 1975), bk. II, chap. XXVII, sec. 26, p. 346.

70. John Locke, *Two Treatises of Government*, ed. Peter Laslett (Cambridge: Cambridge University Press, 1988), II, sec. 27, pp. 287–88.

One need not embrace any particular theory of the relationship of mind and body to know that, certainly under normal circumstances, each person is associated with, or embodied in, one body and one body only. Aristotle makes mention of this principle when he describes "slaves who merit being such by nature," surely a kind of person whose acquaintance he had never made:

> For the same thing is advantageous for the part and the whole and for body and soul, and the slave is a sort of part of the master—a part of his body, as it were, animate yet separate. There is thus a certain advantage—and even affection of slave and master for one another— for those [slaves] who merit being such by nature; but for those who do not merit it in this way but [who are slaves] according to law and by force, the opposite is the case.[71]

Surely Aristotle was aware that the actual slaves he knew were "according to law and by force," and, as he suggests, such slaves do not usually exhibit affection for their masters. Slaves by force are not a part of the master's body but have their own bodies, desires, wishes, and, in general, their own principles of motion. The core of what is one's own is one's body; it is the kernel around which we build our self-identity and extend our personality into the wider world of experience, through acquisition of attachments to other persons and to corporeal things, to causes, and so on. This basic core of what is "one's own" is central to the rights theory of the legal theorist Hugo Grotius; it encompasses one's life, limbs, and liberty, the last being "the power, that we have over ourselves."[72]

One's body is centrally, inescapably connected to one's identity. As *Economist* editor and political theorist Thomas Hodgskin noted,

---

71. Aristotle, *Politics*, 1255b10–15, p. 43.

72. Hugo Grotius, *The Rights of War and Peace*, trans. A. C. Campbell (London: M. Walter Dunne, 1901), bk. I, chap. II, 4, p. 19. Grotius's concept of the "suum"— Latin for "one's own"—is elucidated in Stephen Buckle, *Natural Law and the Theory of Property, Grotius to Hume* (Oxford: Clarendon Press, 1991), pp. 29–52.

Mr. Locke says, that every man has a property in his own person; in fact, individuality—which is signified by the word *own*—cannot be disjoined from the person. Each individual learns his own shape and form, and even the existence of his limbs and body, from seeing and feeling them. These constitute his notion of *personal* identity, both for himself and others; and it is impossible to conceive—it is in fact a contradiction to say—that a man's limbs and body do not belong to himself: for the words him, self, and his body, signify the same material thing.

As we learn the existence of our own bodies from seeing and feeling them, and as we see and feel the bodies of others, we have precisely similar grounds for believing in the individuality or identity of other persons, as for believing in our own identity. The ideas expressed by the words mine and thine, as applied to the produce of labour, are simply then an extended form of the ideas of personal identity and individuality.[73]

Recognition of this fact was central to the liberal tradition, both in Europe and in America. Thus, as Destutt de Tracy noted in a work edited by Thomas Jefferson (and endorsed by Jefferson with his "hearty prayers, that while the Review of Montesquieu, by the same author, is made with us the elementary book of instruction in the principles of civil government, so the present work may be in the particular branch of Political Economy"),

as soon as this individual knows accurately itself, or its moral person, and its capacity to enjoy and to suffer, and to act necessarily, it sees clearly also that this self is the exclusive proprietor of the body which it animates, of the organs which it moves, of all their passions and their actions: for all this finishes and commences with this *self*, exists but by it, is not moved but by its acts, and no other moral person can employ the same instruments nor be affected in the same manner by their effects. The idea of property and of exclusive property arises then necessarily in a sensible being from this alone, that it is suscep-

73. Thomas Hodgskin, *The Natural and Artificial Right of Property Contrasted* (1832; Clifton, N.J.: Augustus M. Kelley, 1973), pp. 28–29.

tible of passion and action, and it arises in such a being because nature
has endowed it with an inevitable and inalienable property, that of its
individuality.[74]

Certainly there are other theories of personal identity that do not
rely on an individual's perception of his limbs and body in order, in
Hodgskin's words, to "constitute his notion of *personal* identity, both
for himself and others."[75] But not all theories of personal identity are

74. The Count Destutt de Tracy, *A Treatise on Political Economy*, trans. Thomas
Jefferson (1817; New York: Augustus M. Kelley, 1970), p. 47. Destutt relates the
institution of several property, or of mine and thine, to the distinction between me
and thee: "[T]he thine and the mine were never invented. They were acknowledged
the day on which we could say *thee* and *me*; and the idea of *me* and *thee* or rather of
me and something *other than me*, has arisen, if not the very day on which a feeling
being has experienced impressions, at least the one on which, in consequence of
these impressions, he has experienced the sentiment of willing, the possibility of
acting, which is a consequence thereof, and a resistance to this sentiment and to
this act. When afterwards among these resisting beings, consequently other than
himself, the feeling and willing being has known that there were some feeling like
himself, it has forced to accord to them a *personality* other than his own, a *self*
other than his own and different from his own. And it always has been impossible,
as it always will be, that that which is *his* should not for him be different from that
which is *theirs*" (p. 49). The "Review of Montesquieu" mentioned by Jefferson is *A
Commentary and Review of Montesquieu's Spirit of Laws*, by Antoine Louis Claude
Destutt de Tracy, trans. Thomas Jefferson (1811; New York: Burt Franklin, 1969).
75. See, for example, the arguments offered on behalf of psychological continuity
as criterion of personal identity in Derek Parfit, *Reasons and Persons* (Oxford: Oxford
University Press, 1986), and those offered by Thomas Nagel in *The View from
Nowhere* (Oxford: Oxford University Press, 1986) on behalf of "the hypothesis that
I am my brain" (p. 40). The "closest continuer" view of identity and the added
concept of the reflexive self-referring of the "self-synthesizing self," advanced by
Robert Nozick in his *Philosophical Explanations* (Cambridge: Harvard University
Press, 1981), are compatible with the view I expound in this essay, insofar as the
"weighted metric" to which I appeal is one suitable to a "social matrix." As Nozick
notes, "[P]roblems of overlap [in applying notions of identity to people] can arise at
one time, given the different possibilities of carving up the world. If you can clump
yourself along any (artificial) relations around reflexive self-referring, can your demarcation of yourself include my arms, or my whole body? Or even my capacity to
reflexively self-refer? Some uniformity of delimitation is achieved in a social matrix.
Rewards and punishments will lead to a boundary in a particular location along given
innate salient features or dimensions. Recalcitrant individuals who act on their

or need be relevant to the formulation of a theory of rights. Theories based on strange hypotheticals and counterfactuals and on nonstandard cases, such as multiple personalities, Siamese twins, or amnesiacs, are unlikely to meet the criteria of publicity and generality necessary for a functional rights theory. "Bodily self-ascription" (to use Gareth Evans's phrase for the principle advanced here), on the other hand, has the marked advantage of "immunity to error through misidentification."[76] As Evans notes,

---

deviant classifications wherein part of their own body includes someone else's arms, will be punished, institutionalized, or killed. Usually, the mutual compatibility of self-definitions occurs with less hardship" (pp. 107–8). See also the consideration of the role of personal identity in assigning responsibility and in the attribution of benefits and obligations in Eddy M. Zemach, "Love Thy Neighbor As Thyself, Or Egoism and Altruism," in *Studies in Ethical Theory*, ed. Peter A. French, Theodore E. Uehling, Jr., and Howard K. Wettstein, Midwest Studies in Philosophy, vol. III (Minneapolis: University of Minnesota Press, 1980), pp. 148–58. Zemach's approach suffers, however, from an excessively nominalist orientation, which, while allowing him to admit that "although everything in nature is, under some classification or other, a part of the agent of any given action *x*, there must be some parts of nature which are closer to *x* than others" (p. 154), keeps him from admitting substances or natural entities that are materially and numerically individuated; were he to admit such entities, individual personal responsibility would be a natural consequence of his analysis.

76. See Gareth Evans, "Self-Identification," in *Self-Knowledge*, ed. Quassim Cassam (Oxford: Oxford University Press, 1994), pp. 184–209. As Evans puts it, the judgment "*a* is F" is immune to error through misidentification if "it is based upon a way of knowing about objects such that it does not make sense for the subject to utter 'Something is F, but is it *a* that is F?' when the first component expresses knowledge which the subject does not think he has, or may have, gained in any other way" [than the normal way]. See Gareth Evans, *The Varieties of Reference*, ed. John McDowell (Oxford: Oxford University Press, 1982), pp. 189–90, quoted in a footnote in Gareth Evans, "Self-Identification," p. 194. The Stoic philosopher Epictetus considered such self-ascription the most certain kind of knowledge. In his response to the skepticism of the Pyrrhonists and the Academic philosophers, Epictetus argued, "But that you and I are not the same persons, I know very certainly. Whence do I get this knowledge? When I want to swallow something, I never take the morsel to that place, but to this." Epictetus, *The Discourses as Reported by Arrian*, vol. I, bk. I–II, trans. W. A. Oldfather (Cambridge: Harvard University Press, 1998), I.27, 18–19, p. 173.

we have what might be described as a general capacity to perceive our own bodies, although this can be broken down into several distinguishable capacities. . . . Each of these modes of perception appears to give rise to judgments which are immune to error through misidentification. None of the following utterances appears to make sense when the first component expresses knowledge gained in the appropriate way: "Someone's legs are crossed, but is it my legs that are crossed?"; "Someone is hot and sticky, but is it I who am hot and sticky?"; "Someone is being pushed, but is it I who am being pushed?" There just does not appear to be a gap between the subject's having information (or appearing to have information), in the appropriate way, that the property of being F is instantiated, and his having information (or appearing to have information) that *he* is F; for him to have, or to appear to have, the information that the property is instantiated just is for it to appear to him that *he* is F.[77]

Each person is identified with one and only one body, spatio-temporally distinct from all others. Each person is a source or principle of motion for one body.[78] Each body provides demarcation of a

77. Gareth Evans, "Self-Identification," p. 198. Evans also allows certain forms of mental self-ascription to be immune from errors of misidentification, for perceptual states "must occur in the context of certain kinds of knowledge and understanding on the part of the subject" (p. 208) that will entail knowledge of a persisting self: "No judgment will have the content of a psychological self-ascription, unless the judger can be regarded as ascribing to himself a property which he can conceive as being satisfied by a being not necessarily himself—a state of affairs which he will have to conceive as involving a persisting subject of experience. He can know that a state of affairs of the relevant type obtains simply by being aware of a tree, but he must conceive the state of affairs that he then knows to obtain as a state of affairs of precisely that type. And this means that he must conceive of himself, the subject to whom the property is ascribed, as a being of the kind which he envisages when he simply envisages *someone* seeing a tree—that is to say, a persisting subject of experience, located in space and time" (p. 208).

78. As Adam Smith notes of "the man of system," "apt to be very wise in his own conceit . . . [and] . . . so enamoured with the supposed beauty of his own ideal plan of government, that he cannot suffer the smallest deviation from any part of it": "He seems to imagine that he can arrange the different members of a great society with as much ease as the hand arranges the different pieces upon a chess-board. He does not consider that the pieces upon the chess-board have no other principle of motion

sphere of "ownness." The values that one acts to attain or preserve
are the values of materially individuated agents; they are "agent-
relative." Each person is responsible for those acts in cases in which
he or she "could have done otherwise." Each person is responsible
for the acts of his or her own body, but not (excepting special cases,
such as guardianship of minors and the mentally deficient) for the
acts of the bodies of others, for these are the responsibility of other
agents—those whose spheres of "ownness" are defined by those bodies.[79]

Recognizing that each person bears responsibility for his or her
acts entails that each person is also obliged to act in accordance with
deontic constraints on behavior. Moving from "normative solipsism"
to "normative pluralism"—from the view that one is the only agent
acting to achieve values in the world to a recognition that one is one
among a multitude of acting agents—need not entail a move from
the agent-relativity of values to the agent-neutrality of values, as some
have asserted,[80] but provides the groundwork for recognition of a

---

besides that which the hand impresses upon them; but that, in the great chess-
board of human society, every single piece has a principle of motion of its own,
altogether different from that which the legislature might chuse to impress upon it."
The Theory of Moral Sentiments (Oxford: Oxford University Press, 1976), pp. 233–
34.

79. As Hugo Grotius notes, "It is the CIVIL law . . . which makes an owner
answerable for the mischief or damage done by his slave, or by his cattle. For in the
eye of natural justice he is not to blame." *The Rights of War and Peace*, bk. II, chap.
XVII, par. XXI, p. 201.

80. This is the claim of Thomas Nagel, regarding at least pleasure and pain, in
The View from Nowhere, pp. 156–62. Nagel claims that the idea that "pleasure is a
good thing and pain is a bad thing" (p. 159) is "self-evident" and that to deny it and
to assert the agent-relativity of all values "is a very peculiar attitude to take toward
the primitive comforts and discomforts of life" (p. 160). I do not find Nagel's claims
convincing, although "something like it" seems to be true. That "something like it"
is to be found in the principle of sympathy (most normal people are concerned about
the welfare, including the pleasures and pains, of others) and in the deontic side
constraints to be discussed in a moment. For a defense of the agent-relativity of all
values, see Eric Mack, "Agent-Relativity of Value, Deontic Restraints, and Self-

deontic constraint on the pursuit of agent-relative values—that the spheres of ownness of others are not to be invaded or usurped in pursuit of one's own agent-relative values.[81] In recognizing that persons bear responsibility for their acts, we are *not* compelled by the structure of practical reason to adopt a special perspective that ranks all values and lives equally from a maximizing perspective, such that an aggregate of equally valid lives or values is what is to be conserved or advanced from some agent-neutral perspective,[82] but we are moved toward a constraint on behavior that affects others.[83] Some have suggested that it would be a failure of deliberative or practical rationality to fail to recognize the equal claims of others or to integrate their values into one's own, but while this is attractive, I see little warrant for it. A far stronger ground for recognizing deontic constraints on behavior is that the realm of responsibility of each individual maps precisely on to a realm of legitimate claims; the fact that each has a life to lead is coextensive in moral significance with the fact that each bears responsibility for acts in a well-delineated sphere of ownness. Each governs in his or her own body; each body has its own principle of motion; each is held by others to be responsible for what he or she

---

Ownership," in *Value, Welfare, and Morality,* ed. R. G. Frey and Christopher W. Morris (Cambridge: Cambridge University Press, 1993), pp. 209–32.

81. See Eric Mack, "Personal Integrity, Practical Recognition, and Rights," *The Monist* 76, no. 1 (January 1993): pp. 101–18.

82. See the discussion of the issues related to such an agent-neutral consequentialism in Samuel Scheffler, *The Rejection of Consequentialism: A Philosophical Investigation of the Considerations Underlying Rival Moral Conceptions* (Oxford: Clarendon Press, 1982). Scheffler attempts to integrate into an agent-neutral consequentialist approach an "agent-centred prerogative" that would allow individuals to avoid pursuing agent-neutral values in certain cases where they might violate the integrity of the agent.

83. Eric Mack, "Personal Integrity, Practical Recognition, and Rights," p. 102: "in general, in such [favorable social and material] circumstances the constraining deontic reason prevails in the sense that, although the value of the ends which the agent seeks is not denigrated, the agent is precluded from obtaining them through the contemplated course of action."

does with that body; the body demarcates that person as an identity, as the same with himself or herself and as different from others; and this body is the seat of the claim to pursue one's *own* values—those with which one identifies as an agent, which give coherence to one's life and integrate one as one person, rather than as simply a random and unintegrated conglomeration of desires.[84]

Precisely because each person has one and only one body, rights over bodies—a "property in one's person"—offer a secure foundation for the entire structure of rights, one that does not necessarily generate conflicts. The starting point is secure. It provides a foundation for a system of "compossible" rights, that is, rights that are capable of being jointly realized.[85]

If a theory of rights generates *in*compossible claims to act legitimately, as do the theories criticized earlier in this essay, that theory generates contradictions as fatal to it as are logical contradictions to a system of mathematics.[86] It is in the nature of "right" that two mutually incompatible actions cannot both be "right"; they may be understandable, or virtuous, or even noble, but both cannot be right and just at the same time and in the same respect. Recall Socrates'

---

84. On the role of value and project pursuit in the attainment of person identity and coherence, see Loren Lomasky, *Persons, Rights, and the Moral Community* (Oxford: Oxford University Press, 1987). As Lomasky notes, "[R]egard for someone as a rights holder is grounded in the recognizability of that being as a distinct individual. It is not *personhood* which calls for respect but rather distinct persons. Between these two conceptions there is a sharp divide, one separating an ethic in which individualism is valued from an ethic subscribing entirely to an impersonal standard of value" (p. 167). Cf. Thomas Nagel ("Equality," in Thomas Nagel, *Mortal Questions* [Cambridge: Cambridge University Press, 1979]): "The concern with what one is doing to whom, as opposed to the concern with what happens, is an important primary source of ethics that is poorly understood" (p. 115).

85. For a fuller explanation of compossibility, see Hillel Steiner, "The Structure of a Theory of Compossible Rights," *Journal of Philosophy* 74 (1977): pp. 767–75.

86. Cf. Hillel Steiner, *An Essay on Rights* (Oxford: Blackwell, 1994), p. 3: "Any justice principle that delivers a set of rights yielding contradictory judgements about the permissibility of a particular action either is unrealizable or (what comes to the same thing) must be modified to be realizable."

warning when discussing justice: "The argument is not about just any question, but about the way one should live."[87] Justice is about which acts are permissible or obligatory and which are not, and rights are the signposts that tell individuals how they may and may not act. Incompossible rights give contradictory information; they are like signposts for "North" that point in opposite direction.

A theory that recognizes the responsibilities and duties of each entails recognition of a set of corresponding rights. As Hillel Steiner notes, "A duty-holder who lacks any rights is one whose liberties are all naked and whose duties may thus be incompossible either with one another or with those of others or both."[88] In order to fulfill our duties, rights are necessary, and if our duties are equal, then these rights are equal rights. The rights to our own spheres of ownness— over that for which we are responsible—is the natural correlative to the obligations associated with the sphere of ownness.[89] And that sphere of ownness defines both rights and duties: it is the right of all persons to themselves, to their own bodies. The obligations derive from the engagement in moral discourse, from the equality involved in the giving of reasons among agents all of whom bear responsibility for their own acts and who have their own lives and purposes, rights derived both from the necessity of avoiding incompossibility of ob-

87. Plato, *The Republic*, trans. Allan Bloom (New York: Basic Books, 1968), 352d, p. 31.

88. Hillel Steiner, *An Essay on Rights*, p. 88. In justification of this claim, Steiner notes immediately before it (pp. 87–88) that "[S]ince (i) a right is entailed by a correlative duty, and (ii) a set of categorically compossible rights is entailed by a set of categorically compossible correlative duties, and (iii) such duties are ones involving the duty-holder's exercise of only his vested liberties, and (iv) vested liberties imply duties of forbearance in others, it follows that *a set of categorically compossible rights implies the presence of rights in duty-holders*: namely, rights correlative to those forbearance duties that conjunctively form the perimeter surrounding any duty-holder's vested liberties."

89. See the discussion of the relationship between duties and rights in John Locke's theory in A. John Simmons, *The Lockean Theory of Rights* (Princeton, N.J.: Princeton University Press, 1992), pp. 72–75.

ligations and duties, extensionally defined, and from the claims of all to live their lives.[90] What defines and makes possible the discharge of obligations and the enjoyment of rights is self-proprietorship, or a "property in one's person."[91]

Property in one's person provides a foundation for a system of compossible rights, which themselves are the juridical structure of a society of freedom and justice. As Kant noted, "Right is . . . the sum total of those conditions within which the will of one person can be reconciled with the will of another in accordance with a universal law of freedom."[92]

Kant recognized quite clearly that what distinguishes the just from the unjust system is the ability of all of the legitimate claims to be exercised at the same time, to be compossible. Objective right has to do with the "sum total" of the acts of persons, not merely "the duties in each individual case," in Waldron's terms; in order for justice and rights (or objective and subjective right) to be complementary, the duties in each individual case can be duties only if the sum total of them yields justice or right. Kant concludes that,

90. Not all rights are directly derivable from obligations, for there are many cases in which one may assert a claim that does not prejudice others, which is neither a necessary condition for fulfilling an obligation nor a forbearance from failing to fulfill an obligation. As Locke notes, every person has from birth "*A Right of Freedom to his Person,* which no other Man has a Power over, but the free Disposal of it lies in himself." John Locke, *Two Treatises of Government,* II, sec. 190, pp. 393–94. Locke asserts that "Wherever others are not 'prejudiced,' 'every man' may consider what suits his own convenience, and follow what course he likes best." As cited in A. John Simmons, *The Lockean Theory of Rights,* p. 77. For a careful exposition and use of the distinction between intensionally described and extensionally described actions, see Hillel Steiner, *An Essay on Rights.*

91. See Steiner, *An Essay on Rights:* "The rights constituting a person's domain are . . . easily conceived as *property rights;* they are (time-indexed) rights to physical things. A set of categorically compossible domains, constituted by a set of property rights, is one in which each person's rights are demarcated in such a way as to be mutually exclusive of every other person's rights" (p. 91).

92. Immanuel Kant, "The Metaphysics of Morals," in *Political Writings,* ed. Hans Reiss (Cambridge: Cambridge University Press, 1992), p. 133.

Every action which by itself or by its maxim enables the freedom of each individual's will to co-exist with the freedom of everyone else in accordance with a universal law is *right*.[93]

I have a right to those actions that are compatible with the equal freedom of all others; the sum total of those actions yields justice.[94]

CONCLUSION

Formulating theories of rights that generate logical chaos and social conflict does not advance rights or justice. Such theories tear asunder rights and justice, eliminating both and substituting for them "human wish," arbitrary power, and violence. In so doing, they undermine the very civilization that justice, law, and rights have made possible.

It is no accident that the traditional view of rights that I have sketched out (quite incompletely, to be sure) motivated the American founding and the formulation of the sets of rights articulated in the Constitution of the United States. The incompatibilities and failures (most strikingly in the case of the injustices and rights violations suffered by African slaves), although clear to some at the time of the founding, took time for their elimination. Practice did not correspond to theory but, partly through the Thirteenth, Fourteenth, and Fifteenth Amendments to the Constitution, were brought into closer correspondence. To this day they remain incompletely correspondent; it is in the nature of morality and justice that they are not always observed, for the simple reason of human choice, which makes possible both virtue and vice, both justice and injustice. Injustices and rights violations will never be completely eliminated, however much

93. Ibid., p. 133.
94. The one basic right, then, is the right to freedom: "Freedom (independence from the constraint of another's will), insofar as it is compatible with the freedom of everyone else in accordance with a universal law, is the one sole and original right that belongs to every human being by virtue of his humanity." Immanuel Kant, *The Metaphysical Elements of Justice*, trans. John Ladd (New York: Macmillan Publishing Co., 1985), pp. 43–44.

we are called to eliminate them. But, unlike the rights theories criticized earlier, a compossible set of rights has the advantage that it can be realized in the most part, that it does not necessarily lead to conflicts and to the abandonment of rights as criteria for deciding conflicts of interest. It is in this way that the project initiated by the American founders—which was in fact a continuation of a wider tradition of European civilization, constitutionalism, and law—reveals its greatest wisdom. That is why the American experiment, even with all its flaws, remains an attractive model for the world.

Recall the wisdom of Aristotle: "It is better if all these things are done in accordance with law rather than in accordance with human wish, as the latter is not a safe standard."[95] The statement is no less true in the twentieth century C.E., a century washed in blood by the arbitrary power of rulers unlimited by secure principles of justice and attached instead to "dynamic," unpredictable, irreconcilable "rights."

95. Aristotle, *Politics* (1272b5–8), p. 80.

CHAPTER THREE

"The State of Nature Has a Law of Nature to Govern It"

Eric Mack

THE DECLARATION OF INDEPENDENCE attributes certain fundamental individual rights to all persons—among them the rights to life, liberty, and the pursuit of happiness. The authors of the Declaration and at least most of those who subscribed to it had a particular understanding of these fundamental rights. They took these rights to be natural in the sense that they were possessed by individuals by virtue of certain basic features of human nature. As they understood it, these rights do not arise from such contingent and reversible conditions as compacts among individuals or decrees of rulers. These rights are not the creatures of political authority; they are temporally antecedent to and, in the order of things, independent of positive law. Moreover, these rights are what Thomas Hobbes termed "rights properly so-called." They are rights that all other individuals and all institutions are morally bound to respect. These natural rights properly so-called define for each individual an original moral domain within which he is free to act as he judges fit; they define a moral space for each into which others may not trespass.

It was understood that free agreement—including the consent that (purportedly) founds political society and government—could modify an individual's original complement of rights. Such agreement could subtract particular rights from or add particular rights to a given individual's inventory of rights and thereby relocate portions of the moral boundaries—the moral "fences"—that define that individual's protected domain. The fundamental rights that the Declaration ascribed to individuals were understood to stand as the starting point—the moral baseline—for reasoning about whether any treatment of any individual impermissibly trespasses upon that individual or is permissibly noninvasive. Since the doctrine of the Declaration is that the general consent that (purportedly) founds political society involves no surrender of the baseline rights of life, liberty, and pursuit of happiness, the moral boundaries defined by those natural rights remain in place even after the establishment of political society. Any infringement of those rights—even (or especially) by government, which, after all, is charged with protecting those rights—is morally illicit. The core (if not sole) purpose of legitimate political power is simply the protection of these natural and retained rights.

The main theoretical purpose of this essay is to sustain the presumption of the Declaration that a crucial component of our original moral condition is our possession of rights properly so-called—rights that others are morally bound to respect. One way of framing the question of whether individuals originally possess rights properly so-called is in terms of the debate between the two great English state of nature theorists, Thomas Hobbes and John Locke. Hobbes denies and Locke asserts that our original rights are rights properly so-called. Hobbes maintains that by nature all individuals possess the right to do *anything* they choose; but, precisely for this reason, no one has by nature any obligation to respect anyone else's rights. In contrast, Locke holds that each individual's natural rights involve correlative natural obligations upon all others not to deprive that person of those rights. According to Locke, it is because people possess state of nature rights, which others are obligated to respect, that "The *state of nature* has a law of nature to govern it, which obliges every one."

(6)[1] This is why, though the state of nature "be a *state of liberty,* yet *it is not a state of license."* (6) In this essay, I will support the Declaration's understanding of our natural rights by presenting a sympathetic account of how Locke, who was the single most important source for the doctrine of the Declaration, defended his contention that the state of nature has a law of nature to govern it.

I shall need to say something more about the contrast between the Hobbesian and the Lockean conception of the rights that persons possess in the state of nature. Before doing so, however, it may be helpful to situate the discussion of the character of our state of nature rights within an overview of the state of nature methodology employed by Locke (and Hobbes) and carried over into the Declaration. State of nature theory investigates part of the original moral condition of individuals living in proximity to one another but in the absence of political authority and, indeed, of all contractual ties. It is concerned with what rights, if any, individuals possess in the state of nature and what fundamental features of human existence support the ascription of original rights to the inhabitants of the state of nature. State of nature theory does not concern itself with, for example, what makes for a virtuous or vicious life—in the state of nature or anywhere else—though it may well concern itself with whether any individual has the right to impose virtue upon another.

State of nature theorists examine the prepolitical (and precontractual) condition of mankind in order to distinguish between the rights

---

1. John Locke, *Two Treatise of Government,* ed. and introduction by Peter Laslett, 2d ed. (Cambridge: Cambridge University Press, 1967). All parenthetical citations in the text indicate paragraph numbers in *The Second Treatise.* Hobbes also employs the language of laws of nature. But Hobbes's laws of nature do not seem to express obligations owed to others; rather they seem to be mere counsels of prudence. For instance, it is a counsel of prudence to seek peace when peace can be attained. See Thomas Hobbes, *Leviathan,* ed. Richard Tuck (Cambridge: Cambridge University Press, 1991), chap. XIV.

and obligations (if any) that people have acquired through bilateral or multilateral agreements or through the actions or decrees of any political authority and the rights and obligations (if any) that people possess independent of such agreements or actions or decrees of authority.

The resulting division between original and acquired rights provides a method for assessing the soundness of any actual attribution of a right. For instance, suppose a right to Joshua's unquestioned obedience is attributed to Rebekah. We should *affirm* this right if either (a) Rebekah would possess this right in the state of nature *and* Rebekah has not actually divested herself of that right by one of the procedures through which one can surrender an original right, by her agreement to waive this right, for example, or (b) Rebekah would not possess this right in the state of nature, *but* she has actually acquired this right by one of the procedures through which one can add to one's complement of rights, by Joshua's agreement to total obedience to Rebekah, for example. We should *reject* the attribution of this right if either (a_1) Rebekah would not possess this right in the state of nature *and* she has not actually acquired this right by one of the procedures through which one can add to one's complement of rights, or (b_1) Rebekah would possess this right in the state of nature, *but* she has actually divested herself of this right by one of the procedures through which one can subtract from one's complement of rights. In the particular case at hand, Locke himself would deny (for reasons we shall be surveying) that Rebekah possesses a state of nature right to Joshua's unquestioned obedience. Rebekah's possession of this right will turn on whether she has actually acquired the right through some procedure adequate to yield this result. According to Locke, for Rebekah to have come into possession of this right Joshua must have agreed to be unconditionally obedient to Rebekah without his having been subject to unjust coercion. Such agreement by Joshua can only occur if Joshua has unjustly aggressed against Rebekah, has come under Rebekah's control, and agrees to be unconditionally obedient to her in order to avoid her just execution of him. (23) Thus, according to Locke, Rebekah's alleged right to Joshua's unconditional obedience should only be affirmed if Joshua has actually agreed to this obedience under these very special circumstances.

Locke himself thought of the state of nature as an actual temporal phase of human existence—a phase in which, according to him, some of the inhabitants of seventeenth-century North America still existed. Nevertheless, the actual temporal existence of the state of nature is not crucial for state of nature theory. Even if people have always instantaneously exited the state of nature by immediately entering into agreements establishing some form or other of political authority over them—so that the state of nature exists only as a theoretical construct—it is still important to know what rights individuals possess in this theoretical state of nature. For this knowledge will reveal to us the moral default position, the inventory of rights properly ascribed to each given individual absent a showing that, through his or her voluntary actions, this individual has added particular rights to or subtracted particular rights from his or her original rights. This knowledge of people's original rights is, thus, crucial to the method just described for assessing any given attribution of a right.

The inquiry into what rights people possess in a state of nature is also part of a larger inquiry into what life would be like for people in the absence of political authority. The investigation of what rights people possess in the state of nature feeds into this larger inquiry because what life would be like for people in the absence of political authority depends *in part* on what rights they possess in that prepolitical condition. Individuals who have one array of rights and who think of themselves and others as possessing these particular rights will interact with one another quite differently from individuals who have a different array of rights and think of themselves and others as possessing those particular rights. If one concludes, as Hobbes does, that individuals in the state of nature possess rights that are actually unlimited, blameless liberties—moral liberties to do any and every thing—one will tend to see the state of nature as a war of all upon all. In contrast, if one concludes, as Locke does, that individuals in the state of nature possess rights that restrict the conduct to which others may subject them, one will tend to see the state of nature as more benign. Of course, what life would be like for people in the state of nature will also depend upon factors less directly connected with what rights people are perceived as having. For instance, everything else being equal, an important factor would be how extensively and stably people are able to cooperate in the absence of political authority.

This larger state of nature inquiry determines whether individuals within the state of nature would face fundamental problems that call upon them to create some specific form of political authority. The idea behind this broader investigation is that, if we want to understand what form of political authority (if any) is legitimate, we should understand what problems (if any) political authority is necessary to solve; and we can only understand this by seeing what problems (if any) individuals would face and be unable to solve in the absence of political authority. An elegant state of nature theory—such as Locke's—is one in which the difficulties facing people in the state of nature—Locke calls them "inconveniences"—are due to their exercise of certain of their original rights, while the solution for these difficulties involves individuals' engaging in a mutual and rights-respecting readjustment of their original rights; and the scope and mandate of the resulting political authority is itself defined in terms of individuals' remaining original or freely acquired rights. More specifically, the doctrine of Locke and of the Declaration is that the inconveniences that exist in the state of nature are due to individuals' separate and uncoordinated exercise of their rights to act as executors of the law of nature, that is, to defend themselves against violations of their rights to life, liberty, and estate and their rights to extract reparation from and punish violators of these rights to life, liberty, and estate. According to this doctrine, the solution to the problems associated with separate and uncoordinated enforcement of the law of nature is the vesting of the rights to defend, impose reparation, and punish in a single agency that has the purpose and contractual obligation to exercise these rights on behalf of the rights retained by individuals—namely, their original and undiminished rights to life, liberty, and estate. The failure of any government to fulfill this contractual obligation to its citizens and, even more seriously, any government's violation of its obligation to respect the original and retained rights of its citizens dissolves any obligation of obedience on the part of the citizenry and justifies their resistance against this morally discredited regime. Crucial to this entire Lockean picture, which is wholly taken over by the Declaration, is the idea that there is a law of nature that governs the state of nature, that this law consists in rights that demand respect, that governments are instituted better to enforce this law, and that any government's authority depends upon its systematically carrying out this task.

Having outlined the significance for Locke and for the Declaration of the assertion that the state of nature has a law of nature that governs it, let us introduce a bit of additional vocabulary for capturing the difference between Hobbesian state of nature rights, which are *not* rights properly so-called, and Lockean state of nature rights, which *are* rights properly so-called. What we want here is the distinction, introduced by Wesley Hohfeld, between "liberty-rights" and "claim-rights."[2] Individual R possesses a liberty-right with respect to individual J to engage in action A if and only if R is not under any (enforceable) obligation to J not to engage in A. Individual R possesses a general liberty-right to engage in action A just in case he or she has no (enforceable) obligation to anyone to eschew action A. So liberty-rights are merely a matter of the absence of obligations. If R possesses a general liberty-right to do A, he or she violates no obli-

---

2. Wesley Newcomb Hohfeld, *Fundamental Legal Conceptions*, ed. Walter Wheeler Cook (New Haven: Yale University Press, 1919).

gations to anyone when A is performed. R is totally *blameless* in the performance of A (at least within the context of the enforceable claims of others). The extent of liberty-rights is inversely related to the extent to which (enforceable) obligations obtain among people. A world totally devoid of (enforceable) obligations is a world in which liberty-rights are most extensive; it is a world in which individuals are blamelessly at liberty to do anything whatsoever. Hobbes's state of nature is such a world; the rights that everyone possesses in that world are simply liberty-rights that reflect the nonexistence of any (enforceable) obligations among the inhabitants of that world. Blameless liberties are not rights properly so-called.

In contrast to R's liberty-rights, R's claim-rights involve correlative (enforceable) obligations upon others. Claim-rights can be characterized either in terms of an agent's having a right to engage in a certain action or an agent's having a right over a certain object. In the first case, if R has a claim-right against J to engage in action A, J has an (enforceable) obligation not to preclude R's engaging in A. In the second case, if R has a claim-right against J to object O, J has an (enforceable) obligation not to interfere with R's disposition of O. There is a tendency in Locke to characterize basic claim-rights as rights to certain objects—albeit "object" is understood broadly; so among the objects one has claim-rights to are one's life, limb, liberty, and possessions. I shall follow this tendency, which better accords with the idea that rights define boundaries or fences protective of an individual's sheltered domain. Each individual's sheltered domain consists of the objects over which that individual has claim-rights. However, many of the rights that we actually cite are really compounds made up of claim-rights and liberty-rights. For example, consider an individual's right to pursue happiness. This right is a compound of the individual's claim-rights over his or her own life, physical endowment, talents, and energies and the various additional means he or she has acquired that might be used in the pursuit of happiness and the individual's liberty-rights to engage happiness-promoting strategy$_1$ or strategy$_2$ or strategy$_n$. (The individual will have a liberty-right to engage in any happiness-promoting strategy that does not violate other people's claim-rights. This means the individual will have a liberty-right to engage in any strategy that does not make use of "objects" within other agents' sheltered domains.)

One can see the compound nature of the right to pursue happiness by imagining an agent who waives one or another of the elements of this compound. First, then, imagine that Rebekah retains her claim-rights over her life, physical endowment, and the like but waives her liberty-right to engage in happiness-promoting strategies by agreeing never to engage in such endeavors. She would, by this admittedly odd agreement, acquire an (enforceable) obligation to others to forgo all these strategies. But she would retain her claim-rights to her life, physical endowment, and the rest in the sense that any seizure or destruction of these objects by others would still violate her rights. Second, imagine that Rebekah does not obligate herself to eschew happiness-promoting strategies, but she does agree to waive her claim-rights over her life, physical endowments, and the rest. She would, in this case, retain her liberty-rights to pursue happiness but deprive herself of the moral boundaries that exclude others from making use of her life, endowments, and the like in their pursuit of happiness. In this case, by shedding her claim-rights, Rebekah would be acquiring the moral standing (or nonstanding) that Hobbes takes us all to have in the state of nature. A world in which the only rights are liberty-rights is a world in which there are no rights properly so-called. Rights properly so-called are claim-rights or compounds of claim-rights and liberty-rights.

Although Hobbes and Locke disagree about the natural existence of rights properly so-called, they share a background premise, which I shall label the "Individualist Thesis." This is the view that the most basic teaching of practical rationality is that each person has reason to advance his or her own good. The Individualist Thesis takes the human good to be, so to speak, privatized; each person's good stands as a separate and distinct ultimate end—an end that particular person has reason to promote. The Thesis as such does not specify of what an individual's good consists. Individual well-being may consist of earthly self-preservation or happiness or eternal salvation. The Thesis merely maintains that, for each individual, his or her own genuine good—whatever that is—is the state of affairs that he or she has reason to promote as an end in itself and not merely as a means to some further end. Notice also that the claim that this proposition is *the most basic teaching* of practical reason may mean either that: (1) this proposition is the most basic truth within the normative realm so that all other normative truths must be derivative from it, or that (2) this proposition is the first *known* normative truth but not necessarily *the* most basic truth. On the second understanding, recognition of the truth of the Individualist Thesis may lead us to knowledge of other, equally fundamental, normative truths.

The acceptance of the Individualist Thesis defines the project of all liberal political theory—or at least all *individualist* liberal political theory. This is the project of showing how the adoption of constraining interpersonal norms—rights and correlative obligations that restrict how individuals may promote their own goals—coheres with or is even supported by the Individualist Thesis. The individualist liberal theorizes that, although the Thesis is the first teaching of practical rationality, this proposition about practical rationality leaves room for or even supports an additional teaching: that all individuals are subject to and protected by constraining interpersonal norms. The basic line of argument is that a due appreciation for the separate moral importance of each individual and (perhaps) the social conditions necessary for the flourishing of separate individuals leads to the conclusion that there are principles of justice or rights that protect each individual from being treated as a means even to the most grandiose collective ends. Despite their different conclusions regarding distributive justice, this general line of thought is present in both John Rawls's *A Theory of Justice* and Robert Nozick's *Anarchy, State, and Utopia* when these authors argue that, to take the separateness of persons seriously, one must not merely reject the idea that individuals exist to serve the collective good but also endorse fundamental rights to liberty that protect each individual's choice about the disposition of his or her own life and liberty.[3] This line of thought is present when Ayn Rand argues that robust individual rights are the appropriate interpersonal principles for a society in which each person rationally seeks individual happiness.[4] And it is present when contractarian theorist David Gauthier argues that the rational path to maximal individual utility is the path of the constrained maximizer who is steadfastly disposed to respect the rights of others.[5] In examining Locke's case for the existence of a law of nature that governs the state of nature, we are examining how and how successfully Locke himself carries out this core project of individualist liberal political theory.[6]

At first blush, it may seem that this project can be readily completed because the Individualist Thesis does point to individuals' having natural rights of *some* sort. For if each individual has reason to promote his or her own ultimate good, it seems that no agent is obligated to forgo the promotion of that good. Hence, each agent has a liberty-right to pursue his or her good. However, the difficult question—as one would expect—is whether each agent's pursuit of that good is in some way protected by claim-rights, that is, by rights

3. John Rawls, *A Theory of Justice* (Cambridge: Harvard University Press, 1971), and Robert Nozick, *Anarchy, State and Utopia* (New York: Basic Books, 1974).

4. Ayn Rand, *The Virtue of Selfishness* (New York: New American Library, 1964), especially "Man's Rights" and "The Nature of Government."

5. David Gauthier, *Morals by Agreement* (Oxford: Oxford University Press, 1986).

6. Other treatments of the individualist liberal project include: Douglas Den Uyl and Douglas Rasmussen, *Liberty and Nature* (LaSalle, Ill.: Open Court, 1991); Loren Lomasky, *Persons, Rights, and the Moral Community* (Oxford: Oxford University Press, 1987); Tibor Machan, *Individuals and Their Rights* (LaSalle, Ill.: Open Court, 1989); and Eric Mack, "Moral Individualism: Agent-Relativity and Deontic Restrictions," *Social Philosophy and Policy* 7, no. 1 (Autumn 1989).

properly so-called. On the one hand, Rebekah's blameless liberty to pursue her good will be effectively advantageous to her only if it is accompanied by claim-rights against others' interfering with her pursuit. On the other hand, if others are precluded from infringing upon Rebekah's pursuit of happiness, these other agents must be constrained in their own pursuit of happiness. There must be some modes of pursuing their own good from which they are morally precluded. But, in light of the Individualist Thesis, how could it be reasonable for any of these individuals, such as Joshua, to accept that there are constraints upon his pursuit of his own good? How could it be reasonable for Joshua to recognize an obligation to Rebekah that delimits his pursuit of his own valuable ends? These are the questions to which there must be good answers if Locke's claim that the state of nature has a law of nature to govern it is to be affirmed.

Locke offers his answer to these questions in the highly condensed discussion of natural rights and natural law in paragraphs 4 through 7 of *The Second Treatise*. We can extract four lines of reasoning from these paragraphs—although, as we shall see, these lines share certain premises. I shall label these: (a) the False Presumption Argument, (b) the Workmanship of God Argument, (c) the Generalization Argument, and (d) the Like Reason Argument. All four arguments are worth considering for the light they throw on the project of grounding belief in a law of nature that governs the state of nature. As we shall see, arguments (c) and (d) provide interesting support for the Declaration's assertion of rights properly so-called.

(a) *The False Presumption Argument.* Aside from sharing the Individualist Thesis, Hobbes and Locke agree that there exists a natural moral equality among all persons. No person is by nature authorized to be the master or owner or ruler of any other person. No person is by nature designated to be the servant or slave or subordinate of any other person. No person is born with a saddle on the back, and no person is born with spurs so as better to ride any other person. Of course, were God to have clearly signaled to us that one person has been anointed the master or owner or ruler of others, we would have to accept that individual's moral superiority. God, however, has provided us with no such signal. Hence, according to Locke, the state of nature is a state of equality,

> wherein all the power and jurisdiction is reciprocal, no one having more than another; there being nothing more evident, than that creatures of the same species and rank, promiscuously born to all the same advantages of nature, and the use of the same faculties, should also be equal one amongst another without subordination or subjection. (4)

Suppose, however, that without provocation Rebekah proceeds to harm Joshua in "his life, health, liberty, or possessions." (6) According to Locke, any such harmful behavior involves Rebekah's presumption that there *is* an order of "*subordination* among us, that may authorize us to destroy one another, as if we were made for one another's uses, as the inferior ranks of creatures are for ours." (6) But, Locke argues, it is false that there exists this presumed order of subordination; it is false that some of us have been made for the purposes of others. Thus, Locke seems to argue, any such unprovoked harmful behavior on the part of Rebekah (or anyone else) is unjustified. Being unjustified, all such behavior is wrong; all such behavior *wrongs* Joshua and all other persons who share his standing as a moral equal. And to say that such harmful behavior wrongs everyone who is subjected to it is to say that each person has a right against it. Each person, therefore, has a right not to be injured in "life, health, liberty, or possessions." These are rights that others do wrong to violate. They are rights properly so-called and, hence, rights constitutive of a law of nature governing the state of nature.

Unfortunately, there is at least one major flaw in this argument. The flaw is its failure to recognize two different senses—a weaker and a stronger sense—in which Rebekah's injuring Joshua may be said to be unjustified. Rebekah's harmful behavior is unjustified in the weaker sense if it lacks sound, positive vindication. Rebekah's harmful behavior is unjustified in the stronger sense if there is a positive basis for holding that her action is to be condemned. It is one thing to conclude that the positive vindication offered for some action is unsound (or even that all positive vindications that might be offered are unsound). It is another and stronger thing to conclude that there is warrant for condemning the action at hand. It could be that, although Rebekah's action is entirely devoid of positive vindication, there is no basis for its moral condemnation. Only if an action is unjustified in the second and stronger sense of there being a basis for its condemnation can one infer from its being unjustified that it is wrong.

Locke's False Presumption Argument envisions a particular positive justification being offered for Rebekah's injurious action—that Joshua is morally subordinate to Rebekah or that Joshua exists for Rebekah's use. Locke then points out that this offered justification is simply not sound—because the presumption it turns on is false. This leaves Rebekah's action unjustified in the weaker sense. Unfortunately, Locke seems to conclude not merely that Rebekah's action is unjustified in this weaker sense but also that it is unjustified in the stronger sense, which implies that the action is wrong.

It is worth noting why we should expect the False Presumption Argument to fail. This argument rests all or almost all of its weight upon the natural moral equality of individuals, in this case, of Rebekah and Joshua. We have seen, however, that the belief in the natural moral equality of individuals does not distinguish Locke's position from that of Hobbes. And Hobbes, it seems quite reasonably, does *not* move from belief in the natural moral equality of individuals to the conclusion that all (or any) individuals possess rights properly so-called—rights against being harmed in their lives, limbs, liberties, and possessions. According to Hobbes, it would be mere pretense for Rebekah to claim that Joshua is naturally subordinate to her or made for her use. It would be laughable for her to press such a claim as a positive justification of her harmful action. At the same time, it would also be mere pretense for Joshua to claim that Rebekah is naturally obligated not to harm him in his life, limb, liberty, and possessions. For, as Hobbes sees it, the natural moral equality of individuals consists in their each being morally at liberty to do anything whatsoever. Thus, Rebekah is morally at liberty to harm Joshua just as Joshua is morally at liberty to harm her. Joshua's moral equality vis-à-vis Rebekah consists of Joshua's not being obligated to submit to Rebekah and, indeed, not being obligated not to initiate assaults upon her. Thus, the moral equality of Rebekah and Joshua—as that equality is understood by Hobbes—shows that Rebekah's injurious conduct is unjustified in the sense of lacking any positive vindication; but rather than showing that the conduct is wrong, it shows that the conduct is perfectly morally permissible.

According to Hobbes, the only presumption that need be ascribed to Rebekah is the presumption that she is at liberty to assault Joshua; and this presumption, says Hobbes, is entirely correct. Of course, Hobbes's belief that the natural moral equality of individuals consists in everyone's being morally at liberty to do anything whatsoever may be mistaken. Locke's view is that this natural moral equality consists of each having rights properly so-called over his own life, limb, liberty, and possessions so that Rebekah's initial assault upon Joshua is wrong. Locke's view may be the correct view, but one cannot infer this view of people's natural moral equality from the premise common to Hobbes and Locke—that there are no natural superiors and no natural subordinates.

(b) *The Workmanship of God Argument.* One way in which Locke supports his contention that we are not made for one another's uses is by claiming that we are each made by God for his use.

> for men being all the workmanship of one omnipotent, and infinitely wise maker; all servants of one sovereign master, sent into the world by his order, and about his business; they are his property, whose

workmanship they are, made to last during his, not one another's pleasure. (6)

According to this argument, Rebekah's harming Joshua in his life, limb, or liberty—setting aside Joshua's possessions, which are at least further removed from God's workmanship—is wrong because in so acting Rebekah trespasses upon *God's* sheltered domain; in so acting Rebekah is violating *God's* claim-rights. The problem with this argument *for Locke* is that it simply does not have the result that Locke wants. Locke wants Rebekah's harmful action to count as wronging *Joshua*; he wants to establish a doctrine of natural *human* rights, not a doctrine of God's supernatural rights. Although, for Locke, God may be ultimately responsible for the nature that human beings have, it is supposed to be in virtue of this nature that humans possess original rights against one another.

Locke has a couple of secondary reasons for being attracted to the Workmanship of God Argument. Taking note of these reasons helps to explain why Locke appeals to this argument even though it does not serve his primary purpose of supporting natural human rights. Firstly, Locke is eager to deny that children are the workmanship of their fathers (or even their parents jointly). For this would point to children as the property of their fathers (or their parents jointly); and Locke rejects the doctrine of paternal ownership. Declaring that we are all the workmanship of God and, hence, the property of God is a way of avoiding the natural subordination *among* humans that, Locke thinks, would be implied by some of us being the workmanship of others of us.[7] Secondly, Locke is eager to assert that it is not within any individual's moral power to alienate his or her own life or liberty. The reason for this is that Locke wants to have a powerful response to the contention that long long ago—presumably before the time of any recorded documents—people alienated their lives and liberties to political authority. He wants to be able to rebut this contention by

7. See Locke's *First Treatise*, par. 52–55.

saying that people *could not* have alienated these rights because it has never been within their moral power to do so. The proposition that each is actually the property of God puts Locke in position to make this response.[8] For, if our lives and liberty have actually always been God's property, then it has never been within anybody's moral power to alienate his or her life and liberty to political authority. (The Declaration itself substitutes the right to pursue happiness for the more standard right of property, not out of lack of enthusiasm for the rights of property, but rather in order to focus entirely on rights thought to be inalienable.)

(c) *The Generalization Argument.* Within his argumentation for the law of nature, Locke presents a long quotation from "the judicious Hooker," according to which one cannot expect the love of other men if one does not grant them one's own love. (5)[9] The Hooker passage can be read in two ways. On the first reading, we have a proposition of social psychology; one will not be successful at soliciting the love of others unless one acts lovingly toward them. On the second reading, we have a proposition about the logic of normative claims; if one lays claim to certain treatment from other persons, one must grant that these other persons have an equal claim to that treatment from oneself. This seems to be the reading of Hooker on which Locke models his Generalization Argument. A major part of Locke's repeated insistence that we are all "furnished with like faculties, sharing all in one community of nature" (6) and, hence, are all of equal moral standing is that each individual must attribute to all other persons whatever moral rights one (reasonably) attributes to oneself. And,

8. "no man can, by agreement, pass over to another that which he hath not in himself, a power over his own life." (24) For an assessment, in the context of Locke, of the coherence of the idea of rights that one cannot alienate, see Eric Mack, "The Alienability of Lockean Natural Rights," in *Persons and Their Bodies*, ed. M. J. Cherry (Lanchester, U.K.: Kluver, 1999), pp. 143–76.

9. The passage is from Richard Hooker's *Of the Laws of Ecclesiasticall Politie*, bk. I, chap. VIII, par. 7.

according to Locke, the right that each of us reasonably ascribes to ourself is the right to freedom. For each of us rationally desires our own self-preservation; and the behavior on the part of others that endangers our own self-preservation is their intrusion upon our freedom.

> I have reason to conclude, that he who would get me into his power without my consent, would use me as he pleased when he got me there, and destroy me too when he had a fancy to it. . . . To be free is the only security of my preservation; and reason bids me look on him, as an enemy to my preservation, who would take away that *freedom* which is the fence to it. (17)[10]

Here, of course, one's freedom consists in one's marshaling and directing one's own life, limb, liberty, and possessions toward one's own ends.

The Generalization Argument, therefore, asserts both: (a) if one ascribes to oneself a claim-right to one's own life, limb, liberty, and possessions, one must likewise ascribe to each other person claim-rights to their own lives, limbs, liberties, and possessions; *and* (b) even in light of this necessity to ascribe like claim-rights to others, it is *still* rational for one to ascribe this claim-right to oneself. To affirm (b) is to affirm that each person (or at least each person who is not radically aberrant) is better off in a world in which each person's liberty-rights are constrained by each other person's claim-rights over his or her own life, limb, liberty, and possessions than in a world in which no one's liberty-rights are constrained. Everyone (except perhaps for the most aberrant) is better off in a world of constrained liberty than he or she would be in a world of unconstrained liberty. This is to say that it is advantageous for everyone (except the most aberrant) that the state of nature has a law of nature to govern it.

The most obvious reason for this is that the cost to a given indi-

10. Cf. "I have no reason to suppose, that he, who would *take away my liberty*, would not, when he had me in his power, take away every thing else." (18)

vidual of constraining his or her behavior toward others is extraordinarily likely to be less than the benefit to him or her of others'
constraining their behavior toward that individual in a like manner.
Rebekah loses less from not preying opportunistically upon Joshua
than she gains by Joshua's forgoing similar predation upon her.
Among other things, through their reciprocally refraining from predation, they both save on the cost of offensive weapons, defensive
fortifications, and the time devoted to honing their martial skills. The
less obvious reason is that each individual gains from its being known
to others that he or she abides by constraints in conduct toward
others—including constraints against fraud and the nonfulfillment
of contracts. For it is only by being known to others as one who is
disposed to abide by constraints that one will be known to others as
a person with whom they will be able to establish stable, peaceful,
and mutually beneficial relationships. Being constrained in one's
conduct does not merely earn one others' reciprocal restraint, but it
also profoundly enhances the prospects for one's positively beneficial
interaction with others. Rebekah gains from Joshua's being obligated
to constrain his behavior toward her. But the price she pays for this—
namely, being herself subject to like constraints—is not really a price
at all. For she also *gains* from herself being bound to forgo preying
upon, defrauding, and breaking her promises to Joshua. This makes
her a candidate for all those beneficial interactions with Joshua.
(Rebekah also gains from Joshua and Mary being obligated to forgo
predation, fraud, and the like against one another. This sets the stage
for a wider environment of increasingly articulated, mutually beneficial interactions through which Rebekah will reap further benefits.)

If people did start out in the state of nature with mere liberty-
rights, each would, with an eye to self-preservation and happiness,
rationally agree to be subject to constraints against interference with
those liberty-rights. Each, that is to say, would rationally agree to the
conversion of those mere liberty-rights into rights properly so-called.
Each would rationally agree to the establishment of a Lockean law

of nature. According to one characterization of contractarian moral theory, sound interpersonal norms are precisely those norms to which rational individuals *would* agree. So one can find a line of reasoning within the Generalization Argument that is highly congenial to this sort of moral contractarianism. Rights to life, limb, liberty, and possessions and their correlative obligations are sound interpersonal norms because each rational individual would agree to these norms.

Nevertheless, I am not proposing that we read the Generalization Argument in Locke as an expression of moral contractarianism. For, within Locke's argument, it is important that people *actually do* rationally lay claim to rights over their own lives, limbs, liberties, and possessions and, thereby, become committed to acknowledging like rights for all other morally equal beings. Locke may believe that all people actually lay claim to rights for themselves and, thereby, are rationally committed to abiding by others' like rights. If so, it would follow that *any* individual who intrudes upon another's life, limb, liberty, or possessions violates constraints to which he or she has become rationally committed. Such a person violates the law of nature, which that person has, so to speak, legislated for himself or herself.

However, if Locke's Generalization Argument puts such substantial weight upon people's actually attributing claim-rights to themselves and, thereby, being committed to recognizing others' like rights, we have to ask how troublesome it would be for Locke if it should be true that some people do not actually ascribe claim-rights to themselves. We can, in fact, envision two types of cases in which an individual does not actually ascribe rights to himself or herself and, therefore, is not thereby rationally committed to like rights in others. In the first type of case, we have individuals who would be rational to claim rights for themselves even at the "cost" of being bound to abide by others' like rights but who *irrationally* do not claim such rights. In the second type of case, we have "aberrant" individuals who, because of their special predatory or free-riding capacities, may do better for themselves by not being party to the general system of reciprocal restraint and who therefore *rationally* do not ascribe to themselves rights properly so-called.

Instances of the first type can be minimized by better explaining to (nonaberrant) individuals the advantages of a life of mutual constraint. But some such cases may persist—perhaps among individuals too dull or impulsive to grasp these explanations. And there remain cases of the second sort. *As far as the Generalization Argument goes*, Locke must simply say that we are in a state of unconstrained liberty with respect to any such individuals. They are not *obligated* to respect our lives, limbs, liberties, or possessions—but we are entirely free to do whatever is necessary to defend ourselves against them. And, of course, the teaching of the Individualist Thesis is that we *ought* to do whatever is necessary to so defend ourselves. In short, those (if any) who have not committed themselves to the acknowledgment of our rights may, when they threaten us, be killed

> for the same reason that [one] may kill a *wolf* or a *lion*; because such men are not under the ties of the commonlaw of reason, have no other rule, but that of force and violence, and so may be treated as beasts of prey, those dangerous and noxious creatures, that will be sure to destroy [one] whenever [one] falls into their power. (16)

(d) *The Like Reason Argument.* The basic sound conclusion of the Generalization Argument is that the law of nature obtains among all rational nonaberrant individuals. But it obtains among them because they have each legislated it in the sense of having become rationally committed to recognizing one another as bearers of the same claim-rights each asserts for himself. However, this seems to leave the existence of the law of nature more contingent upon particular human decisions than Locke intends. It also seems, contrary to Locke's intentions, to leave some individuals—those who do not ascribe claim-rights to themselves—not subject to the law of nature, even if they are subject to being treated like wolves and lions. The law of nature, after all, "obliges *every one* . . . and reason, which is that law, teaches *all* mankind [that] *no one* ought to harm another in his life, health, liberty, or possessions." (6, emphasis added)

It seems that, to sustain his judgment about the law of nature, Locke needs an argument that does not make people's being subject to that law contingent upon their actually ascribing rights to themselves and, thereby, committing themselves to recognizing like rights in others. Locke provides such an argument at the end of paragraph 6 of *The Second Treatise.*

> Every one, as he is *bound to preserve himself,* and not quit his station wilfully, so by the like reason, when his own preservation comes not in competition, ought he, as much as he can, *to preserve the rest of mankind,* and may not unless it be to do justice on an offender, take away, or impair the life, or what tends to the preservation of the life, the liberty, health, limb, or goods of another.

This is an easily misunderstood passage. Let us first dispose of the misunderstanding and then advance to a correct reading of this argument. At least in the first portion of this passage, Locke seems to be arguing that, just as Rebekah should devote herself to her self-preservation, she should also—"by the like reason"—devote herself to the preservation of others. Locke appears to embrace a utilitarianism of human preservation according to which everyone's preservation is the real end that each individual should serve. Contrary to the Individualist Thesis, individuals should not ultimately aim at their *own* well-being but rather at the aggregate well-being. Rebekah should eschew attacks upon the life, limb, liberty, and possessions of Joshua because such attacks tend to diminish aggregate human preservation. To say that others have rights against such attacks is, on this understanding, to say that such attacks tend to reduce the overall preservation of mankind.[11] The sole exception to impartiality

---

11. An extensive defense of the view—which I reject here—that Locke endorsed norms on the basis of the tendency of compliance with them to promote aggregate

between one's own preservation and that of others is that one is allowed (or required) to give priority to one's own preservation when it comes "in competition" with the preservation of others.

This, however, cannot be the correct reading of this passage. For, according to Locke, that everyone is bound to preserve *himself or herself* is a bedrock feature of the normative order. Each individual has a special responsibility for his or her own life just as, according to Locke, "the care of each man's salvation belongs only to himself."[12] This individuation of people's ultimate ends is deeply embedded in the representation of the state of nature as a condition in which each agent quite properly seeks the preservation of his or her own life, limb, liberty, and possessions. Each individual's responsibility for the preservation of his or her own life is primary; it is not merely the first application we notice of a more basic and general responsibility that everyone has to preserve everyone. It is not that we first notice that Rebekah should preserve herself, and then we recognize that this is merely a truncated and misleadingly narrow implication of the principle that Rebekah should preserve everyone. (Indeed, if Rebekah's being bound to preserve herself were simply one application of a general obligation to preserve everyone, there would be no basis for Locke's saying that Rebekah should give priority to her own life whenever the preservation of other lives comes into competition with it.) So when Locke says that each ought to preserve himself or herself and "by the like reason" preserve the rest of mankind, he cannot be saying that the preservation of each other person joins Rebekah's self-preservation as part of the aggregate end that Rebekah ought to promote.

This idea is confirmed as soon as we notice how Locke explicates an agent's being bound to preserve the rest of mankind. Locke says

---

human well-being is offered by A. John Simmons, *The Lockean Theory of Rights* (Princeton, N.J.: Princeton University Press, 1992).

12. John Locke, *A Letter Concerning Toleration* (Buffalo, N.Y.: Prometheus Press, 1990), p. 57.

that being bound to preserve the rest of mankind means that one "may not unless it be to do justice on an offender, take away, or impair the life, or what tends to the preservation of the life, the liberty, health, limb, or goods of another." (6) And Locke quickly adds that "the law of nature . . . which willeth the peace and *preservation of all mankind*" is observed when men are "restrained from invading others rights, and from doing hurt to one another." (7) The obligation to preserve the rest of mankind consists in the obligation not to injure others in their lives, limbs, and so on—unless they be offenders. The preservation of two individuals comes in competition when an offender violates this law of nature by attacking another's life, limb, liberty, or possessions. The innocent party may then bring damaging force to bear upon the attacker. This is not because this damaging force increases the aggregate of human preservation; rather it is because the attacker wrongly transgresses the law of nature. (7, 8) What matters here is the difference between being innocent and being a transgressor, not the extent of human preservation. A single innocent individual may, if necessary, defend himself by taking the forfeited lives of the many offenders who have killed another innocent person or who are now threatening this innocent individual.

What then is involved in Locke's claim that each Rebekah is bound to preserve herself and "by the like reason" each must eschew injuring others in their lives, limbs, liberties, and possessions? I take Locke to be saying that Rebekah must in her behavior take due cognizance of the fact that all other persons also are not merely blamelessly at liberty to preserve themselves but are also morally bound to preserve themselves; she must take due cognizance of the fact that each has an end of his or her own to which he or she is rational to devote his or her life. We can distinguish between three views about what constitutes Rebekah's being duly cognizant of this normative truth about other people. (i) The *pure strategy view* is that, for Rebekah to be duly cognizant of the fact that other persons are beings with rational ends of their own, she has to notice that it may be *tricky* to make use of those persons for her own purposes. Individuals who have rational ends of their own are more difficult to manipulate and more likely to resist exploitation. On view (i), Rebekah is duly cognizant of others' possession of rational ends of their own if she makes appropriate strategic adjustments in her predatory behavior. On view (i), Rebekah should treat these other beings as though they were made for her use but with the recognition that she is likely to have to be more cunning than when she treats a tree or a sheep as a means to her own ends. (ii) The *constraint view* is that, for Rebekah to be duly cognizant of the fact that other persons are beings with rational ends of their own to which they are properly devoted, Rebekah has to constrain her conduct toward them. Rebekah has to abstain from actions that employ these other beings as means to her own goals. She has to abstain from advancing her own preservation by way of actions that injure others in their capacity to devote their lives, limbs, liberties, or possessions toward their own preservation. (iii) The *conflation view* is that, for Rebekah to be duly cognizant of the fact that other persons are beings with rational ends of their own to which they are properly devoted, Rebekah has to make their preservation an object of her devotion. Everyone's proper ends are to be conflated into a single aggregate end to which everyone is to devote themselves.

I take Locke's position to be that the constraint view is the plausible understanding of the significance for Rebekah of the moral reality that there are other beings who, as much as Rebekah, ought to devote their lives, limbs, liberties, and possessions to their own preservation. The constraint view is the golden mean between view (i), the mistaken insistence that, even though there are these other beings with ultimate ends of their own, it is still appropriate for Rebekah to treat these beings as means to her own ends, and view (iii), the mistaken belief—which appears within that misreading of Locke—that all ultimate ends must be incorporated within a single system of ends to which everyone should be devoted. Only view (ii) takes seriously both the existence of other beings with rational ends of their own by acknowledging that such beings are not available for Rebekah's use "as the inferior ranks of creatures are" (6) *and* the separateness of those ends from Rebekah's so that Rebekah herself is not obligated to serve them. Hence, the law of nature, which provides all individuals with moral immunity in their nontrespassing attempts to achieve their own good, is the appropriate set of interpersonal norms for a world in which no individual is morally subordinate to any other or to any collection of others and each, quite properly, devotes himself or herself to his or her own self-preservation. It is the specification of what is required for individuals to be duly cognizant in their treatment of others of the Individualist Thesis's affirmation of each individual's devotion of himself or herself to his or her own rational ends. If it is rational to endorse the Individualist Thesis, it is rational by like reason to endorse the Lockean law of nature—a law that serves the interests of all except the most aberrant individuals. This means that it is rational to endorse the structure of natural rights asserted by John Locke and by the Declaration of Independence.

CHAPTER FOUR

Why Individual Rights?

Douglas B. Rasmussen

"Rights" are a moral concept—the concept that pro-
vides a logical transition from the principles guiding
an individual's actions to the principles guiding his
relationship with others—the concept that preserves
and protects individual morality in a social context—
the link between the moral code of a man and the
legal code of a society—between ethics and politics.
Individual rights are the means of subordinating
society to moral law.   —Ayn Rand

THE AMERICAN DECLARATION OF INDEPENDENCE is probably the
most famous political expression of the idea that individuals have a
right to liberty. There are, of course, alternative interpretations of
this revolutionary document and this right, but I am not concerned
with these issues. My concern is theoretical. I am concerned with
the argument justifying that individuals have a basic, negative, moral
right to liberty. Why are their such individual rights?

Within the confines of this essay, I cannot provide a complete
answer to this question. However, I can provide an outline of an
argument. This will be my central task. Before doing so, however, I
will first explain what is involved in the assertion that individuals

The generous support of the Earhart Foundation helped make this essay possible.

have a basic, negative, moral right to liberty. Second, I will note the central problem this claim faces. After doing this, I will take up the challenge of providing the framework of an argument in favor of this basic right.

BASIC RIGHT TO LIBERTY

Let us consider the assertion that individuals have a basic, negative, moral right to liberty. "Right" is used here to refer to a claim or entitlement that individuals have on how others will treat them. "Moral" means that this treatment *ought* to exist but not necessarily *does* exist. "Negative" refers to the type of treatment that others owe individuals—that is, they may *not* use individuals without their consent. Specifically, persons are prohibited from initiating, or threatening to initiate, physical force in any or all its forms against other persons. This right is considered *basic* in the sense that it is not founded on any other right and is the source for other, derivative rights—for example, contractual rights.

An individual's right to liberty is also understood to entail two corollary rights: the right to life and the right to private property. So understood, this implies that the lives and resources, as well as conduct, of individuals may not be directed to purposes to which they have not consented. These rights apply to every human person, but they also require a legal system for their actual implementation.

The most important and controversial feature about individual rights is that they override or "trump" all other moral claims. If individuals have a right to liberty, then they may not be physically compelled or coerced to take actions that are in themselves morally worthwhile. Individuals may not be compelled or coerced to engage in actions that, for example, constitute virtuous behavior, or fulfill their moral obligations to others, or achieve the political common good, or promote the greatest good for the greatest number. Further, individuals may not be coercively prohibited from doing what is morally wrong. People ought to be free *to choose* the morally wrong course of action. Physical compulsion and coercion may be used only in defense against or in response to the exercise of physical force or coercion. This is generally understood to include extortion, fraud, or any form of nonconsensual use of persons and their property.

The central problem faced by any advocate of individual rights is how to justify giving the right to liberty such fundamental importance. Why is the right to liberty more important than being virtuous, fulfilling our obligations to others, achieving the political common good, or promoting the greatest good for the greatest number? Any argument on behalf of individual rights must answer this question if it is to succeed.

There are numerous responses to this question. They take various forms and represent a significant part of the literature of contemporary political philosophy. Nevertheless, I will not examine this literature. Rather, I will concentrate on an argument for the individual right to liberty that a colleague[1] and I have developed.[2] This argument at least has the virtue of being quite different from those usually found in rights literature. It seeks to make individual rights the primary political principle, while acknowledging that they are not the primary ethical principle.

1. Douglas J. Den Uyl.
2. This essay uses, develops, and expands upon material from the following: Douglas B. Rasmussen and Douglas J. Den Uyl, *Liberty and Nature* (La Salle, Ill.: Open Court, 1991); idem., *Liberalism Defended: The Challenge of Post-Modernity* (Cheltenham, U.K., and Lyme, U.S.: Edward Elgar, 1997); idem., "'Rights' as MetaNormative Principles," in *Liberty for the 21st Century*, ed. Tibor R. Machan and Douglas B. Rasmussen (Lanham, Md.: Rowman & Littlefield, 1995), 59–75. See also Douglas B. Rasmussen, "Human Flourishing and the Appeal of Human Nature," *Social Philosophy & Policy* 16 (winter 1999): 1–43.

RIGHTS AS METANORMATIVE PRINCIPLES

The basic character of individual rights is not grasped so long as this ethical concept is seen as being of the same *type* as those generally found in normative ethics. Individual rights are a unique ethical concept that cannot be reduced to other normative concepts. Individual rights are not needed in order to know the nature of human flourishing or virtue, or our obligations to others, or even the requirements of justice. Rather, individual rights are needed to solve a problem that is uniquely political and legal. I call it "liberalism's problem," and it can be stated as follows: How do we allow for the possibility that individuals might flourish in different ways (in different communities and cultures) without creating moral conflict? How do we find a political/legal context that will *in principle* not require the human flourishing of *any* person or group to be preferred to others?

An individual's right to liberty is crucial to the resolution of liberalism's problem. By protecting liberty, the possibility of agency or self-direction, which is central to any and every form of human flourishing, is socially preserved. The moral propriety of individualism and the need for sociality are reconciled. An individual's right to liberty is thus not merely a normative principle. Rather, it is a *metanormative* principle—that is to say, it is concerned with the creation, interpretation, and evaluation of a political/legal context.

The rationale behind an individual's right to liberty is the search for a political/legal backdrop that will allow the individual and interpersonal character of the moral life not to be in principled conflict. The legitimacy of this metanormative conception of individual rights as well as the argument for it depends on human flourishing's being (1) objective, but highly individualized (and thus plural), (2) profoundly social, and (3) self-directed. This conception of the human good is crucial to understanding both the moral force and limits of individual rights.

HUMAN FLOURISHING — OBJECTIVE BUT PLURAL

Despite what many contemporary thinkers believe, human flourishing is not merely conventional. Rather, our nature as human beings reveals a cluster of generic goods that we need to have fulfilled in order to flourish. These goods constitute human flourishing. Among these are sociability, knowledge, leisure, aesthetic appreciation, creativity, moral virtue, health, pleasure, self-esteem, and practical wisdom.[3] A human life that fails to partake in some form of each of these generic goods is deficient. Accordingly, human flourishing is not simply a matter of social mores or personal desire. It is our objective good and moral purpose.

These generic goods comprise human flourishing. Each of these goods is necessary to the very character of human flourishing. Yet, when considered as such, without regard to whose goods they are, no one of these generic goods is of any more importance than any of the others. Abstractly considered, human nature does not tell us what weighting or valuation to give to these goods. Contrary to what Plato and Aristotle seem to contend, we do not know the universally best form of human flourishing. There is no general recipe that gives *the* proper valuations or weightings for generic goods that every individual should have. Our moral purpose lies in creating a flourishing life for ourselves, but appeal to abstract moral principles alone or lists of generic goods will not tell us what we need to know. Such ethical rationalism is highly limited.

Indeed, since our humanity is not some amorphous, undifferentiated universal, human flourishing is not something abstract and universal. The generic goods that constitute human flourishing only

---

3. Practical wisdom is the central integrating virtue of human flourishing and as such is present in every virtuous act and generic good. Thus, it and moral virtue (when considered as a whole) are not on the same order as the other generic goods. See Douglas J. Den Uyl, *The Virtue of Prudence* (New York: Peter Lang, 1991). Also see "Human Flourishing and the Appeal of Human Nature."

become real, determinate, and valuable when they are given particular form by the choices of flesh and blood persons. In reality, the importance or value of these goods is rooted in factors that are unique to each person. The circumstances, talents, endowments, interests, beliefs, and histories that descriptively characterize each individual—what is called an individual's "nexus"—determine, as much as possible, the appropriate valuation or weighting of these generic goods for each individual. Human flourishing is not simply achieved and enjoyed by individuals but is itself individualized.

Contrary to the views of most modern ethical theorists, the ethical or moral life requires that persons be *partial* in their valuations of generic goods. The excellent use of practical reason, what Aristotle called *phronêsis* (practical wisdom), requires that individuals discover how a generic good, along with the other generic goods, is to be coherently achieved *in their lives*. This process requires that generic goods not be valued equally but given different valuations or weightings. The value or weight that is accorded a generic good in some individual's life is crucially dependent on that individual's "nexus." The contingent and particular are ineliminable features of the ethical or moral life, and they are essential for determining the proper balance or weighting of generic goods for an individual.

There are individuative as well as generic potentialities, and this makes human flourishing always unique. Moreover, it must be emphasized that human flourishing does not merely occur within an individual's life, as if an individual were simply a placeholder. The generic goods of human flourishing are always goods *for* some individual or other, but the relationship of these goods to the individual is not merely extrinsic. These goods involve an essential reference to the individual for whom they are goods as part of their description. Their value is found and expended in those activities of an individual that constitute his or her flourishing. Human flourishing is agent-relative[4] as well as individualized.

---

4. Human flourishing, G, for a person, P, is agent-relative if and only if its

We can and indeed should consider these generic goods abstractly. However, we should always guard against the temptation to imagine the goods that comprise human flourishing as existing or having value apart from the individuals whose goods they are. Further, we should not imagine individuals as mere placeholders or loci in which these goods are instantiated. Individuals are not metaphysical pincushions in which these generic goods are "stuck," and individuals do more than locate these generic goods in space. It is, to repeat, only through an individual's practical choices that these generic goods become determinate, real, and valuable.

An ethics of human flourishing is a version of moral pluralism. Human flourishing is neither a "Platonic" form nor an impersonal[5] good. There are many forms of human flourishing, but there is no single best form of human flourishing *period*. Rather, there is only the best form of human flourishing *for* an individual.[6] Thus, there are many *summa bona*. Nonetheless, this does not require that human flourishing be subjective. Human flourishing neither consists in merely having favorable feelings nor in having value conferred upon it simply by someone's preference. This individualized account of human flourishing offers diversity without subjectivism.

---

distinctive presence in world W1 is a basis for P ranking W1 over W2, even though G may not be the basis for *any other* persons ranking W1 over W2. See Eric Mack, "Moral Individualism, Agent-Relativity and Deonic Restraints," *Social Philosophy and Policy* 7 (autumn 1989): 81–111.

5. An ethical theory is impersonal when all ultimately morally salient values, reasons, and rankings are "agent-neutral"; they are agent-neutral when they do *not* involve as part of their description an essential reference to the person for whom the value or reason exists or the ranking is correct. "For any value, reason or ranking V, if a person P1 is justified in holding V, then so are P2-Pn under appropriately similar conditions. . . . On an agent-neutral conception it is impossible to weight more heavily or at all, V, simply because it is one's own value." Den Uyl, *The Virtue of Prudence*, p. 27. Accordingly, when it comes to describing a value, reason, or ranking, it does not ethically matter whose value, reason, or ranking it is.

6. In fact, for some persons, especially when they are young and usually before they have made crucial choices, it is possible that there is no single best form of flourishing for them, but rather a limited set of such forms.

HUMAN FLOURISHING — PROFOUNDLY SOCIAL

Human flourishing is not atomistic but highly social. We do not flourish like mushrooms, suddenly, all at once, with no engagement with one another. Rather, our maturation requires a life with others. We have potentialities that are other-oriented, and we cannot find fulfillment without their actualization. Having other-concern (*philia*) is in fact one of the generic goods that comprise human flourishing.

In terms of origin, we are almost always born into a society or community, and it is in some social context or other that we grow and develop. Much of what is crucial to our self-conception and fundamental values is dependent on our upbringing and environment. Our lives are intertwined with others. Indeed, we cannot flourish without societies and communities in which there are shared values. We need to live and work with others according to some common set of values. Therefore, to think that human beings can flourish independently and apart from others commits the fallacy of reification just as much as thinking that human nature or society can exist independently and apart from individuals. Being *a*social is not a policy consistent with human flourishing, and individuals ought to be concerned with the nature of and conditions for social life.

Of course, the need for community life does not necessarily mean that individuals must accept the status quo. It is also true that the community's values should be truly good for the individual. They should not be blindly accepted. It may thus be necessary for persons to leave their community or to change it. Yet, this cannot be done if sociality is only possible with those with whom one currently has common values. It must be possible for persons to have relationships with others with whom there is only a potential for shared values. That is to say, it must be possible for there to be relationships with others where all that is known is that one is dealing with another human being.

Contrary to what seems to have been the traditional Aristotelian view,[7] however, human sociality need not be confined to a select group or pool of human beings. Though relationships with others are founded on common values that form the basis for a continuum of relations—from those with close friends and acquaintances to those with fellow members of communities and cultures—human sociality is open-ended. It imposes no a priori limitation regarding with whom one may have a relationship. To claim, then, that one's flourishing or moral maturation is impossible without sharing values with others does not mean that sociality is confined to only those currently existing relationships and sets of values. Human sociality allows for openness to strangers or human beings in general. Indeed, human flourishing is possible only if people can be open to relationships with others with whom no values are *as yet* shared.

The open-ended character of human sociality is important. It reveals the need for a perspective that is broad enough to explain how the possible relationships among persons who as yet share no common values and are strangers to each other can, nonetheless, be ethically compossible. In other words, it requires that attention be given to how it might be possible for different individuals to flourish and to do so in different ways (in different communities and cultures) without creating moral conflict. Thus, the open-ended character of human sociality requires that any ethics that sees human flourishing as always lived in some community and culture must consider questions concerning the proper character of political/legal orders. Specifically, it requires ethics of human flourishing to consider the question of finding a political framework that is both compatible with the moral propriety of individualism and yet based on something that can be mutually worthwhile for everyone involved. Moreover, since our sociality is essential to our self-understanding and well being, this

---

7. See Julia Annas, *The Morality of Happiness* (New York: Oxford University Press, 1993), pp. 250–52, for a discussion of this point.

concern for political frameworks is not ethically optional for the individual.

When interpersonal or social life is understood as concerned with relationships with *any* human being, and when the individualized and agent-relative character of human flourishing is grasped, then the need for a different type of ethical norm is recognized. What is needed is a norm that is concerned *not* with the guidance of individual conduct in moral activity but rather with the regulation of conduct so that conditions might be obtained whereby morally significant action can take place. The open-ended character of our natural sociality creates the need for a principle that will, as previously noted, allow for the possibility that individuals might flourish in different ways (in different communities and cultures) without creating moral conflict. We need a solution to liberalism's problem. We need a *metanormative* principle.

REQUIREMENTS FOR METANORMATIVITY

We cannot have a metanormative principle that will structurally prejudice the political/legal order of society more toward some forms of human flourishing than others. To do so would make such a principle inconsistent with our claim that human flourishing is the basic moral purpose of every individual. Thus, the principle we arrive at must be universal in the sense of being equally applicable to all individuals. In addition, the universality requirement necessitates that we center our principle on that characteristic present in all forms of human flourishing (or its pursuit). Otherwise, we will again prejudice the situation in favor of some forms of human flourishing over others.

Generic goods will not suffice as our standard here. Although they are universal in the sense of helping to define human flourishing for all individuals, their particular form or weighting varies from individual to individual. We do not possess a priori, universal rules that dictate *the* proper weighting of the generic goods of human flourishing. There is no such thing as agent-neutral[8] human flourishing. This means that while, for example, artistic pursuit or creativity or friendship may be necessary for anyone's flourishing, their particular form or weighting will differ from person to person. Generic goods only have determinacy, reality, and value in relation to the individual. This is the crucial insight of moral individualism or pluralism.

A metanormative principle must apply to both the particular and general in the same way and in the same respect, or we will be back to an a priori slanting of the situation in favor of some forms of human flourishing over others. Of course, it is very difficult to find a candidate for grounding a metanormative principle—one that is retained across individuals and throughout the developmental process of achieving and maintaining individualized human flourishing. Can there be a political/legal order that will *not* require, as a matter of principle, that some form of human flourishing be preferred? How are we to avoid the anarchist's condemnation of political/legal life as necessarily requiring the sacrifice of some form of the good life to other forms? Can we justify a political/legal order? To put the issue graphically, do political/legal orders require moral cannibalism?

JUSTIFYING THE POLITICAL/LEGAL ORDER

The two basic questions of political philosophy are, Is there a connection between the ethical order and the political/legal order? and, If so, what is the nature of the connection between them? If there is no ethical basis for a society's political/legal order, then its legitimacy and authority are dubious. Of course, it might be the case that there can be no morally legitimate political/legal orders.

Yet, even if it is granted that there is some connection between the two, it certainly should not be assumed at the outset that there

8. See notes 4 and 5.

is a direct or isomorphic relation between the two orders, much less an identity. To say that some activity X-ing is morally right or good and ought to be done does not, by itself, imply that X-ing ought to be politically/legally required. Further, to say that X-ing is morally wrong and ought not to be done does not, by itself, imply that X-ing ought to be politically/legally prohibited. Further, these claims are obviously not semantically equivalent. Indeed, as Aquinas notes, there is a difference between demands of justice that are morally binding and the demands of justice that are morally *and* legally binding. It thus cannot be legitimately assumed that politics is simply ethics writ large.

There needs to be something that connects the ethical and the political/legal orders. Indeed, this is, *de jure*, the fundamental *datum explanandum* of political philosophy, and it is incumbent on the political philosopher to show what justifies moving from one order to the next. This cannot be merely assumed. The onus of proof is on the person who seeks to move from the ethical to the political/legal.

As already noted, it is the central aim of this essay to show that an ethics of human flourishing supports an individual's right to liberty and that this right offers, by and large, the best solution to liberalism's problem. Given the previous two paragraphs, it should also be apparent that this argument for the right to liberty is an attempt to find a principled justification for the political/legal order. That is to say, an ethics that conceives of human flourishing as the ultimate moral standard upholds a political/legal order that sees protection of individual liberty as its chief aim. Contrary to many contemporary liberals and conservatives, an ethics of human flourishing or self-perfection does not require a perfectionist politics. The aim of politics is not human flourishing but peace and order (as defined by our basic, negative, moral right to liberty). In other words, there is a perfectionistic basis for a nonperfectionist politics. The key to this argument is the self-directed character of human flourishing because it promises to provide the basis for solving liberalism's problem.

HUMAN FLOURISHING —
A SELF-DIRECTED ACTIVITY

Regarding Aristotle's conception of human flourishing (*eudaimonia*), Jennifer Whiting has made the following comparison:

> A heart which, owing to some deficiency in its natural processes, cannot beat on its own but is made to beat by means of a pacemaker is not a healthy heart. For *it*, the heart, is not strictly performing its function. Similarly, a man who, owing to some deficiency in his natural capacities, cannot manage his own life but is managed by means of another's deliberating and ordering him is not *eudaimôn*—not even if he possess the same goods and engages in the same first order activities as does a *eudaimôn* man. For *he*, the man, is not strictly speaking performing his function. . . . Aristotle's claim that *eudaimonia* is an activity of the soul in accordance with virtue shows that he thinks that *eudaimonia consists in* exercising rational agency.[9]

Regardless of what Aristotle's position may ultimately be, Whiting's comparison is apt. Human flourishing is fundamentally a self-directed activity.

Human flourishing must be attained through an individual's own efforts and cannot be the result of factors that are beyond one's control. Flourishing does not consist in the mere possession and use of needed goods. Rather, human flourishing consists in a person taking charge of his or her own life so as to develop and maintain those virtues that will, in most cases, achieve the needed goods.

The point here is not, however, that self-direction is merely necessary for the *existence* of human flourishing, for surely there are numerous such necessary conditions. Self-direction is not simply one of those many conditions. The point is rather that self-direction is necessary to the very *essence* of human flourishing. Self-direction is the central necessary constituent or ingredient of human flourishing.

9. Jennifer Whiting, "Aristotle's Function Argument: A Defense," *Ancient Philosophy* 8 (1988): 43.

No other feature could be a constituent or ingredient without self-direction. In other words, self-direction is both a necessary condition for, and an operating condition of, the pursuit and achievement of human flourishing. Regardless of the level of achievement or specificity, self-direction is a feature of all acts of human flourishing. Self-direction is what makes human flourishing an activity.

To appreciate fully this understanding of self-direction, we need to consider briefly the role of practical wisdom as the central integrating virtue of human flourishing. Since there are no a priori, universal rules that dictate the proper weighting of the goods and virtues of human flourishing, a proper weighting is only achieved by individuals having practical insight at the time of action. They need to discover the proper balance *for themselves*. The generic goods of flourishing need to be achieved, maintained, and enjoyed in a coherent manner. Practical wisdom is the ability of the individual at the time of action to discern in particular and contingent circumstances what is morally required. Practical wisdom is practical reason properly used.

In sum, practical wisdom is the intelligent management of one's life so that all the necessary goods and virtues are coherently achieved, maintained, and enjoyed in a manner that is appropriate for the individual human being. Yet, this exercise of practical reason is not automatic. Regardless of one's level of learning or degree of ability, effort or exertion is required. One must be active, not passive, to discover the goods and virtues of human flourishing as well as to achieve and implement them.

The act of using one's intellectual capacity is an exercise of self-direction, and the act of self-direction is an exercise of reason.[10] They are not separate acts of two isolated capacities but distinct aspects

10. See Den Uyl, *The Virtue of Prudence*, pp. 183–86.

of the same conscious act.[11] Though the conclusions of practical reasoning can be shared, the act of reasoning that is an exercise of self-direction cannot. It is something each person must do for him- or herself. Thus, if we were to speak of "human flourishing" as the "perfection" of the human being, then it would be fundamentally a process of *self*-perfection—where the individual human being is both the agent and the object of the process.

To understand better the overall point of this section, it might prove helpful to consider a thought-experiment inspired by Whiting's comparison. What if human beings were attached to machines that satisfied their every need and thus made it unnecessary for them to do anything? What if everything were done for them so that they were essentially passive? Would their lives be worthwhile? There would be no self-direction, no reason, and no individualization. Fundamentally, their lives would not really be their own. There would be no such thing as human flourishing. Human flourishing cannot be human flourishing if it is not self-directed.

SELF-DIRECTION AS THE
BASIS FOR METANORMATIVITY

Self-direction is both central and necessary to the nature of human flourishing. It is the only feature of human flourishing that is common to all acts of human flourishing and peculiar to each and yet at the same time does not imply any particular form of flourishing. It expresses the fundamental core of human flourishing.

Self-direction meets the requirements for metanormativity. It is the only feature of human flourishing of which it can be said that each and every person in the concrete situation has a necessary stake.

---

11. Aquinas states that "man is master of his actions through his reason and will; whence, too, the free-will is defined as 'the faculty and will of reason.'" *Summa Theologiae*, IaIIae, 1.1.

Further, it is the only feature of human flourishing whose protection is consistent with the diverse forms of human flourishing.

The protection of self-direction is something that, in principle, everyone can fulfill. Further, since it is not only common to but also is required by all forms of human flourishing (or its pursuit), regardless of the level of achievement or specificity, it can be used to create a political/legal order. It does not require that the flourishing of any person or group be sacrificed to any other. Self-direction is thus the one and only feature of human flourishing upon which to base a solution to liberalism's problem.

Self-direction also provides the moral basis for linking the ethical and the political/legal orders. Before ever addressing questions about what one should reason about or how one should conduct oneself, an analysis of the nature of human flourishing reveals that one should think and act for oneself, that is, be self-directed. Simply stated, individuals need to exercise their reason. They need to be self-directed. It is, of course, seldom the case that one ever confronts the issue of exercising one's reason or intelligence as such. We reason about, pass judgment on, give priority to some issue or object; and so this abstract point about the fundamental importance of self-direction to the nature of human flourishing is rarely faced in ethical conduct. Yet, since neither speculative nor practical reason simply occur "naturally," the primary importance of self-direction becomes more apparent when abstracted from specific contexts and applied to the issue of justifying political/legal orders.

It is important to realize, however, that "self-direction" in this context does not mean full-blown Millean autonomy or the directedness of the perfected self where one is fully rational. Instead, it simply means the use of reason and judgment upon the world in an effort to understand and to act within or upon one's surroundings. Self-direction as just described is still true of the actions of the most self-perfected of individuals, but nothing in this description requires or implies such individuals or even successful conduct. Thus, the political/legal order can have an ethical grounding without requiring such an order to be moralistic.

To reiterate, the protection of self-direction as just described does not favor one form of human flourishing over any other because it is the act of exercising practical reason that is being protected, not the achievement of its object. Further, self-direction is not something disconnected from an individual's own good but a necessary component of its achievement. It is the key to solving liberalism's problem.

PROTECTING THE POSSIBILITY OF
SELF-DIRECTION AMONG OTHERS

Self-direction cannot exist when some people use others without their consent. Moreover, since the initiation of physical force is the single most basic and threatening encroachment upon self-direction, the aim of the individual right to liberty is to ban legally such activity in all its forms. The individual right to liberty allows each person a sphere of freedom whereby self-directed activities can be exercised without being invaded by others. This translates socially into a principle of maximum compossible and equal freedom for all.

The freedom must be equal, in the sense that it must allow for the possibility of diverse modes of flourishing and therefore must not be structurally biased in favor of some forms of flourishing over others. The freedom must be compossible, meaning that the exercise of self-directed activity by one person must not encroach upon and does not diminish that of another. Thus, a theory of individual rights that protects persons' self-direction can be used to create a political/legal order that will not necessarily require that the flourishing of any person or group be sacrificed to any other.

By protecting the possibility of self-direction, the right to liberty serves human flourishing, not in the sense of directly and positively promoting it, but rather by preventing encroachments upon the condition under which human flourishing can exist. The aim of the right to liberty is to secure the possibility of human flourishing, but in a very specific way: *through seeking to protect the possibility of self-direction*. In this way, the right to liberty is justified by an appeal to the nature of human flourishing, and a solution to liberalism's problem is provided.

It is important to realize that the individual right to liberty is not directly concerned with the promotion of human flourishing itself, but is concerned only with the condition for it. It is thus not the consequences per se that determine when someone's liberty is violated. What is decisive is whether the action taken by one person toward another secures that other's consent or is otherwise a function of that other's choices. For one may violate another's rights and produce a chain of events that lead to consequences that could be said to be to that other's apparent or real benefit. Alternatively, one may not violate another's rights and produce a chain of events that lead to one's apparent or real detriment. Yet, since the purpose here is to structure a political principle that protects the condition for human flourishing among others, rather than leading to human flourishing itself, the consequences of actions are of little importance (except insofar as they threaten the condition that rights were designed to protect in the first place). The concern here is not with how acts will turn out but rather with setting the appropriate foundation for the taking of any action in the first place.

UNDERSTANDING INDIVIDUAL RIGHTS

Individual rights are not normative principles in the sense of guiding us toward the achievement of moral excellence or human flourishing. Contrary to appearances, they are not ordinary interpersonal normative principles either. Individual rights express a type of moral principle that must obtain if we are to reconcile our natural sociality with diverse forms of flourishing. In other words, we need a robust social life, but we also need to succeed as individuals approaching a particular form of flourishing.

Norms that specify how to live among others and the obligations one is likely to incur in such a life are one thing; norms that define the setting for such interactions and obligations are quite another. The "obligations" one has to another in the latter case are due to a shared need to act in a peaceful and orderly social/political context. These are metanorms. The obligations one has in the former case are a function of what is needed to live well and cannot be generated apart from the particular actions, context, culture, traditions, intentions, and practices in which one finds oneself acting. Those actions and contexts call forth evaluative norms by which success, propriety, and merit can be measured and judged in particular cases. Individual rights are metanorms. They are not, however, *called upon* by the progress of a culture or individual, but rather *depended upon*. As such, individual rights are politically primary.

Individual rights are not, however, primary ethical principles. Failure to see the difference between the function of individual rights and that of other normative principles has been responsible for much of the misdirected criticism of individual rights. Communitarian and conservative critics have, for example, argued that rights cannot be politically primary if they are dependent on some more basic ethical principle. They have also argued that rights cannot adequately handle the complexities of moral life because finer conceptual tools than rights are required. Finally, they have argued that a political regime based on the individual right to liberty requires greater moral foundation than liberty alone to sustain it.

These charges have been dealt with elsewhere,[12] but the reply to all of these charges is simply that they fail to show that the individual right to liberty is not politically primary. Individual rights do indeed

---

12. See Rasmussen, "Community versus Liberty?" in *Liberty for the 21st Century*, ed. Machan and Rasmussen, pp. 259–87.

require a deeper ethical foundation, but that does not mean that rights cannot have a unique function. Furthermore, rights are certainly not meant to replace all the other moral concepts we use, and they are, most assuredly, not the concepts to be used in making subtle moral distinctions. Yet, why should this mean that rights should not be primary when it comes to the political/legal order? Finally, a political regime based on the individual's right to liberty does indeed require more than just the right to liberty to sustain it.[13] Yet, once again this does not mean that when it comes to addressing liberalism's problem, which is indeed the problem of political philosophy, that individual rights are not primary. It is perfectly possible for individual rights to be the answer to a very crucial ethical question without its also being true that individual rights are the answer to *all* ethical questions.

WHY INDIVIDUAL RIGHTS TRUMP

The aim of this essay has been to provide an outline of an argument for individual rights. This has been done. Yet, it still needs to be explained why individual rights override all other moral claims.

First, it should be made clear, if it is not so already, that rights do not override all other moral claims *tout court*. Instead, they only override other claims when it comes to addressing an important but specific problem—what I have called "liberalism's problem." It is only when addressing this problem that individual rights are primary.

Second, the conception of human flourishing that has been presented aims to show the legitimacy and importance of liberalism's problem. A fundamental human problem is that of finding a basis for a political/legal order that will not, as a matter of principle, require that the human flourishing of any person or group be preferred to others. This problem is part of the human condition.

13. See ibid., pp. 282–84.

Third, it cannot just be assumed that politics is simply ethics writ large. Moving from "X-ing ought (ought not) to be done" to "X-ing must be politically/legally required (or prohibited)" requires justification. There needs to be a mediating premise, and this premise needs to be consistent with the highly individualized as well as the profoundly social character of human flourishing. In other words, such a premise needs to meet the requirements of metanormativity. In any political debate or discussion, the burden of proof is on the person who seeks to move from the ethical to the political/legal order.

Fourth, self-direction is both central and necessary to the very nature of human flourishing. It is the one and only feature of human flourishing whose protection by the political/legal order is consistent with the diverse forms of human flourishing. It is also the only feature of human flourishing in which every person in the concrete situation has a necessary stake. It meets the requirements of metanormativity.

Fifth, the individual right to liberty protects the possibility of self-direction in a social context. This in turn secures the *possibility* that individual human beings might flourish in diverse ways in various cultures and communities without requiring that the flourishing of any other individual or group be sacrificed.[14] The individual right to liberty is the solution to liberalism's problem.

Sixth, the individual right to liberty does not guarantee that people will live as they should. It does not even guarantee that people will be self-directed. A political/legal order based on the individual right to liberty is thus nonutopian.

Seventh, the approach to the political/legal order that is required

14. Murder, thievery, rape, extortion, and fraud are legally banned by a political/legal order based on individual rights. Although there might be some individuals who regard these activities as forms of human flourishing, they are not. These activities are incompatible with many of the features of human flourishing but especially the generic good of sociality. Further, to the extent that such activities become a part of "normal" social and cultural practices, then to that extent such societies and cultures are inimical to the social and pluralistic character of human flourishing.

by the individual right to liberty is one that severely limits what such an order may do. This approach rejects the political hubris born of an ethical rationalism that allows political theorists to assume that they can determine what version of human flourishing (or forms of life and culture) should advance or decline. These theorists confuse abstractions with realities, and they forget that the ethical and moral life is lived at the concrete level. They assume they can manage or control society. This is intellectual arrogance.

Eighth, this nonutopian approach to the political/legal order, which is based on the right to liberty, does not take refuge in either ethical conventionalism or nihilism. There are ethical truths, and we do know something about the nature of an individual's self-perfection. Indeed, we know that ethics of individual self-perfection does not require a perfectionistic or moralistic politics.

A MAJOR OBJECTION CONSIDERED

This outline has had to ignore many objections and problems.[15] It is necessary, however, to confront briefly one major objection. This objection is also of a communitarian/conservative nature, and it goes to the very heart of the argument that I have outlined. It simply rejects the distinction between normative and metanormative principles. It claims that the purpose of the political/legal order is to create moral excellence, that it is possible to habituate moral excellence through coercion, and that the political/legal order is ultimately a tool for education. In other words, statecraft is soulcraft.

I will not reprise the discussion of the pluralistic character of human flourishing or indeed the issue of what justifies assuming that one can go directly from the ethical to the political/legal order. Instead, I will respond by noting that the statecraft-is-soulcraft position

15. The relation of justice to the individual right to liberty is a particularly important problem. See Den Uyl and Rasmussen, "'Rights' as MetaNormative Principles," pp. 68–71, for a discussion of this problem.

is guilty of confusing two things: (1) a contingent relationship with a necessary relationship and (2) orderly conduct with moral excellence.

1. It is, of course, possible for coercion to bring some person to a position where they come to understand the appropriateness of a moral norm that they may not have otherwise seen. In fact, the extreme example of this is Solzhenitsyn. He turned the Gulag into an opportunity for moral development. However, there is no necessary relationship here. What examples like the Gulag reveal is that *if individuals have some control over some areas of their lives*, they might be able to integrate their circumstances into their own unique form of flourishing. Yet, what this illustrates is the pluralistic character of human flourishing, not the usefulness of coercion in creating moral excellence. Indeed, what coercion often means for countless persons is the loss of their moral compasses and indeed souls. But numbers do not matter here. What matters here is that coercion is not necessary for attaining moral excellence. If our goal is moral excellence, then there is nothing that recommends coercion.

2. There is a difference between conduct that adheres to a moral norm because one believes it to be appropriate and conduct that proceeds from an understanding of the appropriateness of a moral norm.[16] The latter form of conduct is required for moral excellence. However, understanding the appropriateness of a moral norm requires that the individual exercise both speculative and practical wisdom, but these are essentially self-directed activities. Coercion cannot itself create morally excellent or virtuous persons because it does not ultimately appeal to the understanding or reason of the person to ground his or her belief in the appropriateness of the moral norm. Coercion bypasses the individual's reason.

The communitarian/conservative cannot reasonably hope, there-

---

16. Douglas J. Den Uyl, "Liberalism and Virtue," in *Public Morality, Civic Virtue, and the Problems of Modern Liberalism*, ed. T. William Boxx and Gary M. Quinlivan (Grand Rapids, Mich., Cambridge, U.K.: William B. Eerdmans, 2000), p. 72.

fore, to achieve moral excellence by coercion but must instead settle for orderly conduct. That is to say, the communitarian/conservative has to settle for people's merely believing that some conduct is morally appropriate, not necessarily understanding it. If people come to believe through fear, or the desire to conform, or any other sentiment, that is acceptable for orderly conduct. This is not acceptable, however, for moral excellence or human flourishing.

Despite the rhetoric of moral virtue's appearing to be on the side of those who advocate coercion as a tool for achieving moral excellence, the opposite is the case. It is really the advocate of *liberalism*—that is, a political/legal order that is based on the individual right to liberty—whose position bears the closer relation to moral virtue or excellence. The liberal order may allow people to live lives without virtue or even self-direction. Yet, by limiting itself to context setting (as defined by the individual right to liberty), the liberal order ensures the possibility of moral virtue in a social context for everyone. Alternatively, the nonliberal order, be it of left- or right-wing inspiration, must deny that possibility for some individuals and groups. The truth is that any political/legal order that is not based on the individual right to liberty must practice moral cannibalism to some degree.

CONCLUSION

The American Declaration of Independence changed the landscape of the political world. The implications of the theory of basic, negative, moral rights set forth in that document are still being developed. In many cases, proponents, as well as opponents, of these rights have not grasped their unique nature. I have in this essay tried to do two things. First, I have presented a conception of individual rights that reveals their unique character and fundamental importance. They are metanormative principles. Second, I have provided an outline of an argument for this conception of individual rights. This argument shows how individual rights can be both politically primary but nonetheless dependent on a deeper ethical notion—the concept of human flourishing. Human flourishing is objective, individualized, social, and self-directed. It provides the foundation for the individual right to liberty. There is much more to this story, but this should suffice in giving an initial basis for why there are individual rights.

INDEX

PHILOSOPHIC REFLECTIONS
ON A FREE SOCIETY

Business Ethics in the Global Market
Tibor R. Machan, editor

Education in a Free Society
Tibor R. Machan, editor

Morality and Work
Tibor R. Machan, editor

*Individual Rights Reconsidered: Are the Truths of
the U.S. Declaration of Independence Lasting?*
Tibor R. Machan, editor